Basic English Grammar

LEARN BY DOING

DR. ARUN JEE
Former Principal, Delhi Public Schools
Bathinda, Rajkot & Korba

PRABHAT
PRAKASHAN

Published by
PRABHAT PRAKASHAN PVT. LTD.
4/19 Asaf Ali Road,
New Delhi-110 002 (INDIA)
e-mail: prabhatbooks@gmail.com

ISBN 978-81-961590-6-1
BASIC ENGLISH GRAMMAR
Learn by Doing
by Dr. Arun Jee

Cover Design by:
Ujjawal Kumar

Edition
2025

Price
₹ 300 (Rupees Three Hundred Only)

Printed at
Sita Fine Arts, Delhi

Foreword

Before I started writing this book, I had two questions in mind: Who will be the intended users of the book and how will it be different from other books of English grammar available in the market? The answers to these questions served as a guide in the course of my writing the book. They always kept me on track.

This is a book of basic English grammar for the elementary level of learners. It can even be used for those who want to brush up their basics.

Unlike the prevailing books on grammar in the market the focus of this book is not on learning the definitions of grammatical terms. Instead efforts are made to let the learners identify these items and understand their functions.

The items like nouns, determiners, pronouns, verbs, tenses, adjectives, adverbs are revealed through short and simple sentences both in the examples and exercises. The length and complexity of the sentences used in the exercises increase gradually from two words to three or more as the learner progresses. Rational explanations are given for the learner to understand the rules with ease.

Special care is taken to expose the learners to the unique features of the English language. This is to help them avoid committing common errors. Exercises are prepared to address these errors too. The Answer Key to the exercises are a part of the book.

The book can be used as a course for learners to acquire the basics in grammar.

It may be used as a grammar book for classes 5 to 8 in the CBSE schools and for classes 9 and 10 in the State Board schools in India.

The chapters have been planned in such a way that a learner can get a fair idea of what the ingredients of a simple sentence are. And how these ingredients can be used in the formation of a simple sentence.

Though the book is meant for the learners at the basic level, its sequels will soon be prepared for the intermediate and the advanced level.

Acknowledgments

This book was conceived and nurtured by late Prof Kapil Muni Tiwary, my Guru, without whose guidance I can't imagine how I could complete it. Though he couldn't see the book in print in his lifetime, I have a sense of satisfaction that I have fulfilled the promise I had made to him. I bow in memory of the great soul.

I am indebted to Ms Gayatri Morris, a seasoned English teacher from Rajkot, who went through the manuscript and provided some valuable inputs for its improvement.

I am thankful to all my students, colleagues and teachers who gave me the opportunities of learning the nuances of Grammar in the journey of my career.

Special thanks are due to two of my friends: Social scientist and writer Shrikant as well as literary critic and translator Yadvendra for the encouragement and support.

Words of thanks are not enough for Bandana (wife), Tanmay, Inchara and Medha who have always kept me on toes for this project.

My nonagenarian father has ever been a source of inspiration for me.

Contents

1.
Nouns

Nouns with 's' and without 's'

1.1 Underline the nouns in the two word sentences below. The first one has been done as an example:

a) <u>Birds</u> fly.

b) Bells ring.

c) Flowers bloom.

d) Stars twinkle.

e) Horses neigh.

f) Cars move.

g) Lions roar.

h) Fishes swim.

i) Students study.

j) Athletes run.

k) Plants grow.

l) Clowns perform.

m) Singers sing.

n) Painters paint.

- The words on the left are all naming words called **nouns**.
- The words on the right are action words called **verbs**.
- When **nouns** are with 's', **verbs** are without 's'.

But what happens when **nouns** are without 's' in the sentences below:

Examples:

i) Water boils.

ii) Ice melts.

When the **nouns** are without 's', **verbs** are with 's'.

1.2 Tick the correct choice of the verbs:

a) Accidents occurs/occur.

b) Ink spill/spills.

c) Owls hoots/hoot.

d) Monkeys jump/jumps.

e) Gold shine/shines.

f) Soldiers marches/march.

g) Wood burns/burn.

h) Coal burn/burns.

1.3 Choose the appropriate word from the following to fill in the blanks:

[bite, shouts, play, grows, smiles, passes, study, cries, fall, sticks]

a)	Girls	________	f)	Insects	________
b)	Rohan	________	g)	Mahmood	________
c)	Time	________	h)	Students	________
d)	Apples	________	i)	Grass	________
e)	John	________	j)	Honey	________

1.4 Fill in the blanks using options given:

Nouns are ____________ (naming, action) words and verbs are ___________ (naming, action) words. Nouns ending with 's' take ____________ (nouns, verbs) without 's'. Nouns without 's' take verbs ____________ (with, without) 's'.

2.

Types of Nouns

Common and Proper

Compare the nouns used in the following sentences:

i) Ram comes.

ii) A boy comes.

Ram and *boy* both are nouns. *Ram* is the proper name of a person, while *boy* is the common name of a person. So *Ram* is known as **Proper Noun** and *boy* **Common Noun**. Both *Ram* (Proper Noun) and *boy* (Common Noun) are without 's', so the verb (*comes)*, which is the same in both, has 's'.

Again in each sentence below there are two nouns:

i) Mohan is a friend.

ii) Pune is a city.

In i) *Mohan* is a **Proper Noun** and f*riend* is a **Common Noun.** One is a proper name and the other is a common name for a person.

Similarly in ii) *Pune* is a **Proper Noun** and c*ity* is a **Common Noun.** Each is the name of a place.

2.1 Underline the nouns in the following sentences. Write *P* under Proper Nouns and *C* under Common Nouns. The first one has been done as an example:

a) Moti is a dog.
P C

b) The boy is Ravi.

c) The village is Jaito.

d) Shilpa is a girl.

e) Asia is a continent.

f) The company is Tata.

g) India is a country.

h) The student is Mehak.

i) Priti is a teacher.

j) Roshan is a player.

k) Sherpur is a village.

l) The town is Barh.

m) David is a photographer.

n) Junaid is a worker.

o) Mitthu is a parrot.

Common Nouns have two forms but Proper Nouns have only one.

i) A student plays. → Students play.

In the first sentence, *student* is a common noun. It changes its form here. It becomes *students* in the second sentence. 's' has been added to *student.*

ii) Ali dances. → Not possible to add 's' to *Ali.*

Ali is a proper noun. We can't add 's' to it.

Common Nouns have two forms here. One is with 's' and the other without 's'.

Proper Nouns have only one form.

2.2 Add 's' to the Common Nouns and make the necessary changes accordingly. Remember not to add 's' to the proper nouns. The first and the second have been done as examples:

a) A dog barks. → Dogs bark.
b) Rakesh listens. → Not possible to add 's' to Rakesh
c) A horse runs.
d) India wins.
e) A bird sings.
f) Google sells.
g) A student speaks.
h) Hansa eats.
i) Sunday arrives.
j) A day begins.
k) February comes.

2.3 Fill in the blanks by choosing the correct options:

Nouns can thus be divided into _________ (two, three) types. __________ (Proper, Common) names are known as Proper Nouns and _________(proper, common) names are Common Nouns. Proper Nouns have only ________ (one, two) form. You cannot add 's' to Proper Nouns. But Common Nouns can have _______ (one, two) forms. The words like 'a', 'an' and 'the' can be used before _______ (Proper, Common) Nouns but they are generally not used before _______ (Proper, Common) Nouns.

Common Nouns:

Countable and Uncountable

Some Common Nouns can change their forms but others can't:

i) A teacher writes. → Teachers write.

Teacher is a Common Noun(Countable). It has two forms: *teacher* and *teachers*.

One is with 's', the other is without 's'.

ii) Milk boils. → Not possible to change its form. 's' can't be added to *Milk*.

Milk is also a Common Noun(Uncountable). But it has only one form.

2.4 Add 's' only to the Common Nouns having two forms. Also make other necessary changes:

a) A camel sits. → Camels sit.

b) Coal burns.

c) A farmer walks.

d) A tiger sleeps.

e) Salt dissolves.

f) Oil floats.

g) A train moves.

h) A mango falls.

i) Wind blows.

j) Ice melts.

2.5 Fill in the blanks:

Common Nouns can be divided into ________ (two, three) types. Those which have two forms like girl - girls, tree - trees, goat - goats etc. are known as ___________ (Countable, Uncountable) Nouns. Others like milk, water, salt, sugar etc. have only _________ (one, two) and they are called ___________ (Countable, Uncountable) nouns.

Countable Nouns: Singular and Plural

Look at the following pairs of sentences showing both the forms of Countable Nouns:

i) One <u>bird</u> flies. → Two <u>birds</u> fly.

ii) One <u>student</u> plays. → Three <u>students</u> play.

iii) One <u>car</u> moves. → Many <u>cars</u> move.

2.6 Fill in the blanks using correct forms of the Countable Nouns given in the brackets:

a) One _______ falls. Two ________ fall. (apple)

b) One _______ trumpets. Three _________ trumpet. (elephant)

c) One _______ crawls. Some ________ crawl. (snake)

d) One ______ marches. Many ______ march. (soldier)

e) One ________ sits. Other __________ sit. (passenger)

f) One ________ comes. Several ________ come. (train)

g) One ________ bites. A few __________ bite. (insect)

h) One ________ passes. A number of ______ pass. (day)

i) One ________ rings. Several _________ ring. (bell)

Countable Nouns in the above exercise have two forms: with 's' and without 's'.

apple - apples, elephant - elephants, snake - snakes etc. are Singular in number. But the same with the addition of 's' become Plural. **Singular** is for **one, Plural** for **more than one**.

Plurals: Regular and Irregular

Most Countable Nouns change from singular to plural with the addition of 's' like car – cars, boy – boys, goat – goats etc. but there are others which follow different rules:

Examples:

One man speaks. → Two men speak.

One mouse eats. → Two mice eat.

2.7 The Countable Nouns in the following exercise have been mixed. Some of them change to plural by using 's', while others follow different rules. Fill in the blanks using the correct forms of the nouns given in the brackets accordingly:

a) One _______ arrives. Three _______ arrive. (woman)

b) One _______ ticks. Two ________ tick. (clock)

c) One _______ swims. Many _______ swim. (goose)

d) One _______ opens. A few _______ open. (box)

e) One ______ plays. A number of _______ play. (kid)

f) One ______ falls. Several ________ fall. (orange)

g) One ______ runs. Many ________ run. (child)

h) One ______ grows. More ________ grow. (bush)

i) One ______ grazes. Many ________ graze. (sheep)

j) One ______ comes. Four ________ come. (ox)

k) One ______ falls. Some ________ fall. (leaf)

In the following examples **Plural Nouns** have been changed to **Singular**:

Horses are animals → A horse is an animal. (Horses - a horse, animals -an animal)

Chairs are seats → A chair is a seat. (Chairs - a chair, seats - a seat)

The plural forms, horses, animals, chairs, seats do not take ***a*** or ***an*** but when they are changed to singular they become a horse, an animal, a chair, a seat etc.

2.8 Change the following into singular:

a) Mothers are women.

b) Birds are creatures.

c) Markets are places.

d) Brinjals are vegetables.

e) Wives are women.

f) Children are human beings.

g) Oxen are animals.

h) Mice are living beings.

i) Deer are wild animals.

j) Teachers are human beings.

k) Clocks are machines.

l) Flies are insects.

A or **An** can be used only with **Countable Singular Nouns**. They cannot be used with **Countable Plural, Uncountable or Proper Nouns.**

i) Babies need milk. → A baby needs milk.

(When baby is singular, ***a*** has been used. When it is plural (i.e. babies), ***a*** has not been used. Similarly milk is uncountable, hence it does not take the plural form.

ii) Sehaj likes apples --- Sehaj likes an apple.

(***a/an*** is used when apple is singular. When it is plural(i.e. apples), then ***a/an*** can't be used. Similarly Sehaj is a proper noun, so no ***a/an***)

2.9 Change the following into singular. Make sure *a/an* are used only with Countable Singular Nouns:

a) Obama loves oranges.

b) Students play chess.

c) Goats give milk.

d) Pens require ink.

e) Painters use paint.

f) Snakes eat frogs.

g) Houses need furniture.

h) Sheep eat grass.

i) Gentlemen attend parties.

j) Teeth need care.

k) Ladies wear *sarees*.

l) Men wear *dhotis*.

m) Fish live in water.

n) Babies like toys.

o) Cows feed calves.

p) Deer eat plants.

q) Teddy drinks coffee.

r) Factories create pollution.

s) Maruti produces cars.

t) Google gives apps.

u) Pollution affects cities.

v) Floods hit India.

3.
Pronouns

Look at the following pairs of sentences to understand how the repetition of nouns can be avoided:

i) Ram is a student. Ram goes to school.

   Ram is a student. **He** goes to school

ii) Rani is a player. Rani plays football.

   Rani is a player. **She** plays football.

In the first pair of sentences, ***He*** has been used in place of *Ram* to avoid repetition.

In the second pair, ***She*** has been used in place of *Rani.*

Here ***He*** and ***She*** are used in place of nouns in the above sentences. They are known as **Pronouns**. They belong to a special type of **Pronouns** called **Personal Pronouns**.

The complete list of **Personal Pronouns** is **I, We, You, She, He, It, They.**

3.1 Use the Personal Pronouns (I, We, You, She, He, It, They) to fill in the blanks:

a) Jimmy is a soldier. _______ works in the Indian Army.

b) Hello Anand, _____ am Aditi.

How are ____? Please meet Anuj. _____ is a dancer. The person on his left is Shobha. _____ is a singer. Anuj and Shobha are friends. _____ work together. Today ___ are performing.

c) Sonam has a pet. _____ is a cat. _____ is very fond of her pet. _____ spends a lot of time with _____. Sometimes _____ play together.

d) Do _____ know the story of king Ram?

No, ___ don't.

Ram was the king of Ayodhya. Before _____ became the king _____ had to live in the jungle. _____ lived in the jungle with his wife, Sita, and brother, Laxman.

Sita was innocent. _____ was kidnapped by a king named Ravan. Ram and Laxman became angry. _____ took the help of Hanuman and his friends. _____ attacked the kingdom of Ravan.

Ravan was defeated. _____ was killed. Sita was released. _____ came back home safely.

e) "Hey Raju, Where are _____ going?"

'_____ am going to play hockey.'

'Will _____ let me play too?'

'Why not? Come, _____ will play together.'

f) _____ am Arpan. _____ live with my parents in Pune.

_____ have a younger sister. _____ is a college student.

_____ all live there in a flat. The flat is on the fourth floor. _____ has three rooms.

_____ also have a pet. _____ is a dog. The dog is more attached to my parents. _____ take good care of him.

3.2 Correct the pronouns in the sentences below and write the corrections against each. The first one has been done as an example:

a) Jagat told I. Jagan told me.

b) Us have done the work.

c) The doctor advised he.

d) The teacher spoke to she.

e) Me finished the task.

f) The boys met we.

g) The elephant saw they.

Personal Pronouns before the Verb and after the Verb in a sentence

	Before the Verb (Subject)	After the Verb (Object)
First Person Singular	I	me
Plural	We	us
Second Person	You	you
Third Person Singular(M)	He	him
Singular(F)	She	her
Singular (N)	It	it
Plural	They	them

3.3 Complete the table on the right of these sentences writing the underlined pronouns first. The first has been done as an example:

		Before (subject)	After (object)
a)	Lalan met him.	He	him.
b)	Sonal told me.	______	me
c)	You helped Ravi.	You	______
d)	It came to Sudha.	It	
e)	We played with the children.	We	______
f)	The teacher saw them.	______	them
g)	Vinod spoke to us.	______	us
h)	They ran away.	They	______
i)	I taught English.	I	______
j)	My father wrote to you.	______	you
k)	He learnt the language.	He	______

A **pronoun** is used not just in place of **noun** (one word) but also **a noun phrase** (a group of words with a noun):

Examples:

1. My brother and I met the teacher . → We met him.
2. A tall young man came out to greet Mohan and I. → He came out to greet us.

3.4 Replace the underlined parts of the sentences with suitable personal pronouns. The first one has been done as an example:

a) Setu gave the pen to Rohan. He gave it to him.

b) Baljinder looked at the birds.

c) Maya spoke these words.

d) An elephant was dancing like the boys.

e) You and I should meet the boy and his parents.

f) Sonu and Monu play with my brother and me.

g) Shaheer offered sweets to his mother.

h) My father and mother told stories to my brother every evening.

i) My mother and I showed our house to Shambhu.

j) Sunil and Naveen came to meet my brother.

k) Pranav invited Ranjan and me.

3.5 Change the number of the following sentences: from singular to plural and from plural to singular:

Examples:

i) I am running → We are running.

ii) They are playing. → He / She/It is playing.

a) She is writing.

b) He is speaking.

c) We are trying.

d) They are eating.

e) You are laughing.

f) It is crawling.

g) I am coming.

h) We are running.

i) They are coming.

j) It is singing.

4.
Determiners

Look at the following examples:

a) Tom has <u>a</u> pen.

b) Tom has <u>the</u> pen.

c) Tom has <u>my</u> pen.

d) Tom has <u>this</u> pen.

In the sentences above *a*, *the*, *my* and *this* are the underlined words that have been used before the noun, *pen*. These words determine the scope of the noun. So they are called determiners.

4.1 Use the determiners given in the brackets to fill in the blanks. You may use one determiner more than once:

a) There was _____ king. He had ____ elephant. _____ king liked ____ elephant very much. (the, a, an)

b) Look at _____ book here. It is different from _____ book there. Look at _____ mangoes here. They are bigger than ______ mangoes in the fridge. (these, that, this, those)

c) I have ____ dog. It is _____ friend. Nobody can meet me without ______ permission. (my, a, its)

d) Samarth has _____ pets, _____ rabbit and ____ tortoise. _____ rabbit runs fast. _____ colour is white. But ______ tortoise walks slowly. Samarth likes _____ pets very much. He enjoys _____ company. (the, its, his, a, two, their)

e) I am going to see _____ parents in June ___ year. They are in _____ eighties. They live in ___ eastern part of India. They stay with _____ pair of sparrows in _____ house. (this, their, the, a, my)

f) Ram met ___ sister in Canada. _____ name is Meetu. She lives there with _____ family. They both went to meet _____ parents in the USA. _____ parents have ___ dog. (the, their, a, his, her)

Types of Determiners

Articles: a, an, the

Demonstratives: this, that, these, those

Possessives: my, our, your, his, her, its, their

Numbers: one, two, three etc.

1st, 2nd, 3rd etc.

Quantifiers : much, many, several, some, any, a few, little, a little etc.

Distributive : all, each, every etc.

Articles

A or An: consonant or vowel

4.2 Put the following into singular form:

Example: Fans are appliances → A fan is an appliance.

Plurals	Singular
Fans	a fan

a) Elephants are animals.

b) Hospitals are buildings.

c) Ants are creatures.

d) Geese are birds.

e) Men are human beings.

f) Verbs are words.

g) Cars are vehicles.

h) Indians are Asians.

i) Cats are pets.

j) Apples are fruits.

k) Computers are machines.

l) Oxen are males.

m) Thieves are criminals.

A and ***An*** are **articles** which are used only before countable singular nouns, ***a*** before consonants and ***an*** before vowels.

4.3 Fill in *a* or *an*, where necessary. Put X where *a* or *an* is not necessary. (Clue: Remember to use *a* or *an* only before singular countable nouns).

a) She is doing ____________ homework.

b) ____________ sparrows are flying.

c) ____________ car is coming.

d) ____________ artist is speaking.

e) I am reaching ____________ home.

f) ____________ horses are running.

g) They are watching ____________ movies.

h) ____________ year has twelve months.

i) Would you like ____________ tea or ____________ coffee?

j) I like ____________ sugar.

k) ____________ deer is ____________ wild animal.

l) ____________ fish lives in water.

m) ____________ Malala is from Pakistan.

n) ____________ Pratibha is ____________ photographer.

o) This is ____________ idea.

p) ____________ Parminder is ____________ engineer.

q) ____________ University is ____________ place.

r) He likes ____________ rice and ____________ wheat both.

s) She is coming for ____________ dinner.

t) ____________ lady is ____________ woman.

u) ____________ music is ____________ art.

v) ____________ aeroplane is ____________ mode of ____________ transport.

w) You can use ____________ Facebook as ____________ hobby.

4.4 Fill in the blanks choosing the appropriate words from the box that follows:

We use ***a*** or ***an*** only before Countable Nouns. We cannot use ***a*** or ***an*** before ____________, ____________, or ____________ nouns.

Uncountable, Proper, Countable Plural, Singular

***A*, *An* or *The*: Indefinite or Definite**

The following pairs of sentences show the difference between *a*, *an* and *the*:

i) She is a girl.

ii) She is the girl.

The use of ***a*** before girl makes it indefinite. This means it can be any girl.

However, the use of ***the*** before girl makes it definite. The speaker has a definite girl in mind.

iii) This is an elephant.

iv) This is the elephant.

Similarly, the use of ***an*** before elephant makes it indefinite. It can be any elephant.

But, the use of ***the*** before elephant makes it definite.

4.5 Underline the articles (a, an, the) in the following pairs of sentences and write *I* below the indefinite articles and *D* below the definite article. The first one has been done as an example:

a) Sonu is an engineer.
   I

   Sonu is the engineer.
   D

b) This is the house.

   This is a house.

c) I saw the bird.

   I saw a bird.

d) She has an owl.

   She has the owl.

e) The dog is ill.

   A dog is ill.

f) The ant is climbing.

   An ant is climbing.

g) A bus is moving.

   The bus is moving.

h) I like a song.

   I like the song.

i) This is an umbrella.

   This is the umbrella.

j) The teacher came.

   A teacher came.

a, an both are used before indefinite nouns, ***a*** before consonants and ***an*** before vowels. ***The*** is used before definite nouns.

4.6 Fill in the blanks with *a, an* or *the:*

a) I have _____ house in Mumbai. _______ house is vacant.

b) We went to _______ railway station today.

c) She took _______ hour to reach _______ place.

d) She met _______ English teacher after _____ period.

e) _____ horse is _______ animal.

f) _______ woman was coming towards our house. _______ woman was young.

g) They bought ______ second-hand car yesterday but ________ car looked new.

h) He bought _____ shirt and _____ watch from _______ market. ________ shirt was expensive but ______ watch was cheap.

i) She got _____ bicycle on her birthday. ________ bicycle was made in India.

4.7 Fill in 'the' where necessary. Put X where 'the' is not necessary.

a) He is in _____________ market now.

b) I am reaching _____________ Ambala tomorrow.

c) _____________ lions are ferocious _____________ animals.

d) What is _____________ difference between _____________ stars and _____________ planets?

e) You can learn _____________ cooking with _____________ practice.

f) Both _____________ brothers are working in _____________ same company.

g) All _____________ windows of his house are open.

h) _____________ sky is blue.

i) _____________ President of India is in Delhi.

j) _____________ English teacher was on leave.

k) _____________ earth moves round _____________ sun.

l) He is travelling round ____________ country.

m) When will there be unity in ____________ world?

Generally ***the*** is not used before Proper Nouns. It can be used before Uncountable Nouns, Countable Singular and Plural Nouns.

4.8 Fill in *the* in the following blanks and write the word(s) appearing as clues:

a) I had three pets: a dog, a goat and a cat. ____________ dog died last year, ____________ goat expired last week but ____________ cat is still alive.

b) ____________ book that he bought yesterday is a bestseller.

c) Aman and Ali are two brothers. Aman is ____________ elder one and Ali is ____________ younger.

d) ____________ eldest son of my friend has joined the army.

e) One of ____________ teachers of our school had come to watch ____________ movie.

f) As ____________ lion was old, it died of old age.

g) ____________ student did not attend the school because he was ill.

h) I had three friends. ____________ name of ____________ first one was John, ____________ second one was Mehmood and ____________ third was Ram.

i) He met an elderly gentleman on the platform. ____________ man appeared old and weak.

j) She is ____________ girl who set a record in the Board Exams.

4.9 Fill in 'the', if necessary. Write X in the blank where it is not necessary.

a) ____________ main gate of the house was closed. ____________ windows however, were open.

b) Look here! ____________ book is in my right hand and ____________ pen is in my left hand.

c) What is ____________ source of light on ____________ earth: ____________ sun or ____________ moon?

d) Just as ____________ train started moving from Amritsar, a person entered ____________ compartment.

e) ____________ car had reached Ambala. We were close to ____________ Chandigarh now.

f) ____________ cooking is a skill which can be acquired only through ____________ practice.

g) We begin our day by listening to ____________ twitter of ____________ birds in ____________ morning.

h) ____________ flowers are blooming in ____________ garden.

i) Both ____________ sisters are working in ____________ same company. ____________ elder one is at ____________ Hyderabad while ____________ younger one is in ____________ Delhi.

j) ____________ President of ____________ India is arriving in ____________ city.

Other Determiners:

this that, these those

4.10 Fill in the blanks with either *this* or *that*:

a) Look at _____ book here.

b) _____ mango kept here is sweeter than _____ one on the table.

c) _____ bicycle kept there is mine.

d) _____ chair is more comfortable than _____ one there.

e) _____ key in my hand opens _____ lock there.

f) _____ evening was very enjoyable.

g) I plan to write a story _____ year.

h) Please take _____ bag and keep it on _____ desk there.

i) I don't remember the face of _____ person.

j) Pick up _____ paper and put it in _____ basket at the door.

This is used before a noun to indicate that it is near, while *that* is used before a noun to indicate it is far.

4.11 Based on the examples below change the following into plural:

Examples:

Singular	**Plural**
This orange is fresh. → These oranges are fresh.	
That girl is playing. → Those girls are playing.	
this	these
that	those

a) This story is very interesting.

b) I like that movie.

c) That box is heavy.

d) This boy has broken that chair.

e) That fan is quite old.

f) That student will sit here but this student will stand there.

g) That elephant has broken this plant.

h) He is waiting for that gentleman.

i) She meets this pedestrian.

j) This chapter is easier than that one.

some, any

4.12 Fill in the blanks with either *some* or *any*:

a) There are ______ apples in the bag.

b) Do you have _____ questions?

c) Yes, I have _____ questions.

d) He doesn't have _____ problems.

e) He gave ____ gifts to the children.

f) There are ____ girls in the ground but there aren't _____ boys.

g) Did you get _____ solutions to the problem?

h) No, I haven't got _____ solutions.

i) _____ people came to the house.

4.13 Fill in the blanks with either *some* or *any*:

a) There isn't ____ sugar in the tea.

b) I have _____ juice for you.

c) There isn't ____ water in the pool.

d) _____ milk is required for tea.

e) Is there ____ honey in the bottle?

f) Do you have ____ proof?

g) Yes, I have _____ proof.

h) There isn't _____ oil in the food.

i) But he uses ____ oil for cooking.

Note: *Some* and *any* are used with *Countable* and *Uncountable Nouns* both. _______ (some, any) is used in _______ (affirmative, negative) sentences, while ______ (some, any) is used in ________ (affirmative, negative) sentences and questions.

a few, few, a little, little, much, many

4.14 Fill in the blanks with either *a few* or *a little*:

a) There are _____ students in the class.

b) There is _____ honey in the bottle.

c) ______ passengers got down at the station.

d) Have you seen _____ birds here?

e) There are _____ flowers in my garden.

f) I want _____ butter.

g) Can I have _____ bread?

h) Did you watch ____ movies during your vacation?

i) He has ____ work to finish.

j) Add ___ salt to the salad.

Note: *a few/a little*: number/amount

A few is used with Countable Nouns to express a small ____ (amount, number). *A little* is used with Uncountable Plural Nouns to express a small _____ (amount, number).

4.15 Fill in the blanks with either *much* or *many*:

a) I have ____ bicycles.

b) She doesn't have ____ water for drinking.

c) There are ____ stars in the sky.

d) He got ____ awards.

e) The singer received ____ appreciation.

f) Have you got ____ friends here?

g) ____ people came to the party.

h) They don't have ____ cash.

i) Are they facing ____ problems?

j) No, they aren't facing ____ problems.

k) There isn't ____ fun in the game.

l) She can speak ____ languages.

m) There aren't ____ errors in the book.

n) There wasn't ____ noise in the street.

Note: *much/many*: uncountable/countable

______ (many, much) is used with an **Uncountable Noun** to express a large ____ (amount, number). _____ (many, much) is used with a **Countable Plural Noun** to express a large _____ (amount, number).

4.16 Fill in the blanks with *a few, few, a little, little*:

Examples:

Don't worry, I have ***a few*** bananas for breakfast -- Countable Plural (positive)

I watch ***few*** movies these days because I don't have time -- Countable Plural (negative)

We still have ***a little*** time to finish the homework -- Uncountable (positive)

She has ***little*** education. She can hardly read, write or count -- Uncountable (negative)

a) _____ students from his class read story books, unfortunately.

b) _____ students are interested in chess. You will enjoy playing with them.

c) He is lucky. He has _____ problems.

d) There is _____ milk left in the cup. You can use it for tea.

e) She has _____ time. She rarely talks to her parents.

f) Take out ____ juice from the fridge.

g) I want _____ jam on my bread.

h) If you are interested, I can suggest _____ books on English grammar.

i) I have _____ interest in cricket. It is not a gentleman's game now.

j) He takes _____ care of the house. It is not organized.

k) _____ children come out for games during their exams.

4.17 Use the given determiners to fill in the blanks:

a few, much, many, a little

a) How _____ money do you need?

b) How _____ stories have you read?

c) Only _____ students have come to school.

d) Should I put _____ sugar in the coffee?

e) There is too _____ oil in the vegetable.

f) I don't have _____ friends.

g) How _____ books have you bought?

h) Could you add ____ milk in the tea?

i) He spoke ____ words on the occasion.

4.18 Use a suitable noun from the given box below to fill in each blank:

book, brothers, parents, children, evening, student, hour, information, members, money, sisters, animals, dogs

a) Each _____ received a book.

b) He cares for all _____ .

c) She'll finish the work in half an _____ .

d) He talks to his mother every _____ .

e) All ___ should be checked.

f) I already spent half the _____ .

g) Half of the ___ are not interested in the game.

h) All of my family _____ are coming.

i) Both _____ stay in the same town.

j) Both of my _____ are trained.

k) I can choose either _____ for reading.

l) Either of my _____ is going to see him off.

Determiners or Pronouns?

4.19 In the following pairs of sentences the same word has been used as a pronoun in one sentence and as a determiner in the other. Underline and write *Pr* under the Pronouns and *Det* under the Determiners. One has been done as an example:

a) i) He got that.
Pr

ii) Milan received that gift.
Det

b) i) I have read this book.
ii) I have read this.

c) i) Many birds are sitting.
   ii) Many are sitting.

d) i) They have seen a few.
   ii) They have seen a few trees.

e) i) I ate these apples.
   ii) I ate these.

f) i) She went through some.
   ii) She went through some stories.

g) i) Resham hasn't received any.
   ii) Resham hasn't received any mails.

h) i) Those books are old.
   ii) Those are old.

i) i) Many students are coming.
   ii) Many are coming.

j) i) I have a little milk.
   ii) I have a little.

A **Determiner** is followed by a noun, while a **Pronoun** is not followed by a noun.

→ Personal pronouns can't be used as determiners.

→ Articles (a, an, the) can't be used as pronouns.

5.
Verbs

5.1 Change the following into negative:

Example:

Anju is watching. → Anju is not watching.

a) Babies are crying.

b) Ramu should study.

c) They have reached.

d) Mehar is cooking.

e) Sameer has played.

f) Girls are shouting.

g) You were sleeping.

h) I am walking.

i) He might return.

j) She will explain.

k) Kabir was swimming.

l) Madan had told me.

In this exercise the **verbs** like ***is, am, are, has, have, had, should, will, might, was, were*** are used to make negatives.

5.2 Based on the example given below change the following statements into questions:

He is sitting. → Is he sitting?

a) Raji is standing.

b) They are coming.

c) She can read it.

d) Mukul has gone.

e) They have finished the work.

f) He may speak.

g) Renu was running.

h) Dogs were barking.

i) They will do it.

j) He is listening.

Here again **the verbs** like ***is, are, has, had, can, may, must, will, was, were*** are used to make questions.

Auxiliary and Main Verbs

In the exercises **5.1** and **5.2** each sentence has two verbs. One is an **Auxiliary Verb** and the other is a **Main Verb**. The one that is used for making a negative or a question is an **Auxiliary Verb.** The other one is a **Main Verb**.

A **list** of **Auxiliary Verbs** is as follows:

is, am, are, was, were, has, have, had, do, does, did, will, shall, would, should, can, could, may, might, must, ought to (the list is almost complete).

It is not possible to provide a complete list of **Main Verbs** as they are countless. The **Main Verbs** used in the above exercises are as follows: *cry, study, reach, cook, play, shout, sleep, walk, return, explain, swim, tell, stand, come, read, go, finish, arrive, speak, run, bark, do, write, listen*

5.3 Write AV for the *Auxiliary Verbs* and MV for the *Main Verbs* in the following sentences:

a) They are watching TV.

b) The car started.

c) Birds sing.

d) A boy was running.

e) She told a lie.

f) He will come.

g) You may go.

h) A snake crawls.

i) The game should begin.

j) The bell rings.

k) Students were chatting.

l) The train has arrived.

m) Leaves have fallen.

n) He must get the prize.

o) Both play the game.

p) She can do it.

q) They dance.

Auxiliaries: Primary and Modal

All **Auxiliary Verbs** can be used with **Main Verbs** in sentences. But some are always used **with Main Verbs,** while others can be used both **with Main Verbs** and **without Main Verbs** in sentences.

The auxiliaries that are used both with Main Verbs and without Main Verbs are called **Primary Auxiliaries.**

For example: **Is**

He **is** writing → **is** comes here with the main verb, *writing*.

He **is** Rahul. → Here **is** has been used without a main verb. *Rahul* is not a verb, it is a noun.

The auxiliaries that are used only with Main Verbs are known as **Modal Auxiliaries.**

For example: **Can**

He can dance → with a main verb (dance)

He can *Rahul* → **Not possible**. A main verb is essential with *can. Rahul* is a noun.

Primary Auxiliaries:

is, am, are, was, were, has, have, had, do, does, did

5.4 In the following sentences the Main Verbs have been underlined. Use the Primary Auxiliaries given in the brackets to fill in the blanks:

a) She ______ crying. (am, is, are)
b) We ______ finished the work. (has, have)
c) Rahul _______ not tell lies. (do, does)
d) They ________ singing. (is, am, are)
e) He ________ smiling. (is, am, are)
f) I ________ listening. (am, is, are)
g) It _______ come. (has, have)
h) It _______ running. (is, am, are)
i) We ______ not shout. (do, does)

5.5 In each of the following sentences the Primary Auxiliary has been underlined. If it comes with a Main Verb, then write the Main Verb against the sentence, otherwise write X. The first two have been done as examples:

a) Boys are playing. **playing**
b) The teacher is happy. **X**
c) The school is near.
d) They did it.
e) We have sent the gift.
f) Men are mortal.
g) He did not say anything.

h) They <u>were</u> hungry.
i) They <u>were</u> travelling.
j) She <u>had</u> reached the place.

5.6 A list of Modal Auxiliaries is given below. Use each of them to make a sentence:

will, may, must, shall, might, would, should, can, could, ought to

Examples:

He <u>can</u> lift the bag.

You <u>may</u> come.

5.7 Fill in the blanks using the auxiliaries (Primary and Modal both) given below:

<u>is, has, are, had, does, have, must, do, were, can, should, has, did</u>

a) My grandfather _______ expired that year.
b) Susan _______ ill today.
c) She _______ come.
d) Why _____ you cry?
e) They _____ happy.
f) Both _____ playing.
g) Ramesh ______ join me.
h) Naseer _____ help.
i) He _____ not like it.
j) You _____ listen to me.
k) Alok ______ not respond.
l) Hari _____ replied.
m) We ______ just met.

Main Verbs: Forms/Types

In the following sentences four Main Verbs and their various forms have been used in sentences:

a)	i) They go home.	go
	ii) They <u>went</u> home.	went
	iii) They have <u>gone</u> home.	gone

iv)	They are <u>going</u> home.	going
v)	She <u>goes</u> home.	goes
b) i)	We <u>eat</u> guavas.	eat
ii)	We <u>ate</u> guavas.	ate
iii)	We have <u>eaten</u> guavas.	eaten
iv)	We are <u>eating</u>.	eating
v)	He <u>eats</u> guavas.	eats
c) i)	They open the door.	open
ii)	They opened the door.	opened
iii)	They have opened the door.	opened
iv)	They are opening the door.	opening
v)	He opens the door.	opens
d) i)	They clean the house.	clean
ii)	They cleaned the house.	cleaned
iii)	They have cleaned the house.	cleaned
iv)	They are cleaning the house.	cleaning
v)	He cleans the house.	cleans

Five different forms of these verbs:

V1	V2	**V3**	**V4**	**V5**
go	went	gone	going	goes
eat	ate	eaten	eating	eats
open	opened	opened	opening	opens
clean	cleaned	cleaned	cleaning	cleans

In this table there are variations in V2 and V3 of the Main Verbs. The verbs like *open,* and *clean* change with the addition of 'd', while *go* and *eat* follow different rules.

Thus the verbs like *open, clean* that change to V2 and V3 with the addition of 'd' or 'ed' are known as **Regular Main Verbs,** which are very large in number.

The verbs like *go, eat* that change by following other rules are called **Irregular Main Verbs**.

The first, **V1,** is the base form. The second, **V2,** is the past form. The third, **V3** is known as past participle form. The fourth, **V4**, is the present participle form (**ing** form). The fifth, **V5**, is the 's' form.

V1, is the one by which a main verb is recognized in dictionaries. **V4** (ing form) and **V5** ('s' form) can also be recognized easily as there are no variations in these. The variations occur mainly in **V2** and **V3**. That is why **V1**, **V2** and **V3** remain more in focus for discussion in English grammar.

5.8 Change the Regular Main Verbs used in the following sentences into past form (V2).

Example:

I clean the floor --- I cleaned the floor

a) I call him.

b) They open the door.

c) They dance well.

d) The parents hug her.

e) We decorate the house.

f) The students shout.

g) My teachers advise me.

h) I accept the gift.

i) They close the gate.

j) You behave well.

A list of common **Regular Verbs** is as follows:

accept, admit, add, advise, behave, close, call, clean, dance, discover, decorate, hug, hope, love, melt, move, obtain, open, start

5.9 Change the following into past tense (V2). Remember these are not Regular Verbs. They don't change into past with 'd' or 'ed':

a) They send a gift.

b) I read a book.

c) I feel bad.

d) We buy fruits.
e) You throw the garbage.
f) The parents come.
g) They leave early.
h) We meet in the park.
i) She cuts her finger.
j) I sleep at 10.

A list of common **Irregular Verbs** is as follows:

cut, shut, build, send, feed, lead, read, feel, meet, keep, sleep, leave, buy, bring, think, come, become, know, throw, go, eat, sleep

5.10 Fill in the appropriate forms (V1/V2/V3/V4/V5) of the Main Verbs given in the brackets. They are mixed: some are Regular, some are Irregular.

a) Raju has _______ (become) taller now.
b) I _______ (think) so.
c) Do you ________ (feed) the birds?
d) They _______ (love) trees now.
e) They are ________ (build) a house.
f) The game __________ (start) late.
g) The door is ________ (shut).
h) Amir does not _______ (sleep) on time.
i) Sapna was ______ (admit) to the college.
j) Please ___________ (close) the windows.
k) She had _______ (keep) the promise.
l) He has been ________ (accept) by the group.
m) The students are _________ (decorate) their classroom next week.
n) Ice _________ (melt) due to heat.
o) They have _______ (remove) the garbage.

5.11 Use the appropriate forms of the Main Verbs again to fill in the blanks: (mixed: Regular and Irregular)

a) She has _____________ a paper boat. (make)

b) Rohan ____________ lies. (tell)

c) Brij ____________ correctly last week. (answer)

d) Hasan is ____________ (sing).

e) Mohan ____________ sad today. (look)

f) They were ____________ hard. (work)

g) Manraj was ____________ the school. (leave)

h) They have ____________ friends. (become)

i) She was ____________ by a ball. (hit)

5.12 Underline the Main Verbs in the following sentences and mention if they are *Regular* or *Irregular*. The first has been done as an example:

Example:

I <u>knew</u> the answer. **Irregular**

a) Hari is thinking.

b) She is looking at the sky.

c) Ramu gave me a gift.

d) Manu has asked.

e) Did you find the book?

f) It seems true.

g) He is trying.

h) They are leaving.

i) I want apples.

j) You can see.

k) He will take it.

l) When are you coming?

m) Where is he going?

n) Has she told the truth.

o) They work together.

p) I feel bad.

q) What did they say?

6.
Tenses

Time and Tense

6.1 Read the following sentences and write the tense and the time separately for each sentence. One has been done as an example:

She is reaching next week. **Present Tense – Future time**

a) I have written a story.

b) Bobby has been reading a novel.

c) He will come today.

d) They always come on time.

e) I brush my teeth after breakfast.

f) We finished the work.

g) Sohan is going to help me.

h) He has come.

Tense and Time

Tense is a concept of grammar and **time** is one of life.

Tenses are of three types: Present, Past and Future.

Time also has its three types: Present, Past and Future.

Tenses are used to express the time in life but the relation between time and tense is not always equal.

Examples:

'I am going to Chennai next week' is a sentence in **Present Continuous Tense** but it expresses **future time**.

A sentence in **Simple Present** like 'He wakes up at six' is used to express a habitual action that includes all the time: past, present and future.

Another sentence of **Present Perfect** like 'she has completed the work' is used to express a completed action in the past time.

6.2 Match the sentences on the left with the names of the tenses on the right:

a) He has broken the bat.	Past Perfect
b) Bhushan was reading.	Present Continuous
c) I am sitting.	Past Continuous
d) Geeta brushes her teeth at night.	Simple Future
e) Mohit had informed me.	Future Continuous
f) Rashi has been swimming.	Simple Present
g) Saurabh will meet me today.	Past Perfect
h) They had been trying hard.	Past Perfect Continuous
i) I saw the movie.	Simple Past
j) She will be flying then.	Present Perfect
k) Aman will have reached home.	Future Perfect Continuous
l) Ashu will have been singing.	Future Perfect

Present Tense

Present Continuous: is/am/are + V4(ing)

6.3 Answer the following questions orally. Practise both affirmative and negative answers in complete sentences. See the following as an example:

Question: Is she playing?

Answer: Yes, she is playing. (affirmative) /
No, she isn't playing. (negative)

a) Is he cooking?
b) Are you standing?
c) Am I speaking loudly?
d) Are they listening?
e) Is she driving?
f) Is Reshu waiting?
g) Are we going there?
h) Am I reading correctly?
i) Are you writing an email?
j) Is she running?
k) Are they living here?
l) Are we working together?

6.4 Answer the following questions orally again in complete sentences like the example below:

Question: What are you doing?

Answer : I am eating a mango.

a) What is she writing?
b) What is he reading?
c) Where are we going?
d) What is he eating?
e) Where are you coming from?
f) What are they speaking?
g) What are we carrying?
h) What is she doing?
i) What are you listening to?

j) What are they cutting?

k) Where are you standing?

l) What are you taking?

m) What is he making?

Simple Present: V1/V5 (s/es)

6.5 Answer the following questions orally. An example of a probable answer has been given below for reference:

Question: When do you wake up?

Answer : I wake up at six.

a) When does he go to school?

b) When do they chat?

c) When do you read the textbooks?

d) When does she sing?

e) When does he dance?

f) When do we meet?

g) When does Rohan complete homework?

h) When do we discuss?

i) When does Shweta play hockey?

j) When do they have dinner?

k) When do you brush your teeth?

l) When does he teach?

m) When does your mother call you?

n) When do they ask questions?

o) When does he talk to his friends?

6.6 Read the following in the singular quickly:

a) My daughters play outdoor games.

b) His friends like chicken.

c) They do not like fish.

d) These ladies travel by bus.

e) Her parents do not attend the meetings.

f) They live in big houses.

g) The birds build their nests.

h) The men stay at home, while the women go out for work.

i) The teachers scold the students sometimes.

j) The drivers drive the buses fast.

k) The passengers always arrive late.

6.7 Read the following in the singular quickly:

a) The students start for school in the morning. They attend classes, listen to their teachers, chat with their friends and come back home in the afternoon. In the evening they again go for tuitions and come back tired and exhausted. They don't get the time to play games or self-study.

b) These boys go shopping every Sunday. They purchase vegetables and fruit but they don't buy items like pizza or burgers.

c) Nowadays the children enjoy playing mobile games. They hardly ever go to the parks for outdoor games. It is no surprise then that they suffer from life-style diseases more.

d) They have bananas for breakfast, and we have *chapatis*. For lunch they have rice, we have *dalia*.

e) My cousins study till late in the night. So they do not wake up early in the morning. We finish our work in the evening. So we wake up early.

6.8 Fill in either the Simple Present or Present Continuous forms of the verbs:

(Cues: every day, always, every morning etc, often, sometimes, usually, generally etc.)

a) The sun ________ (rise) in the east.

b) Jameel _________ (watch) TV now.

c) She usually _______ (sing) in Kashmiri but today she ________ (sing) in Punjabi.

d) I _____ (think) he ________ (swim) in the pool at present.

e) The train always _______ (come) on time but today it _________ (come) late.

f) Generally my mother _________ (cook) *chapatis* in the morning but she _______ (cook) *parathas* today.

g) Sonu _____ (read) a novel at present. Otherwise he _________ (play) Football every evening.

h) The teacher never _______ (allow) the students to make fun of others.

i) The birds ________ (build) their nests in the winter.

j) The baby _______ (cry). Probably he _____ (wants) milk.

k) This car _________ (belong) to Mrs. Vatsa. She ___________ (buy) another car next week.

l) I often ________ (meet) him at the corner but today I _________ (meet) him in the office.

m) The lady who ___________ (come) to meet me now _________ (work) for the poor people in this area.

n) "Where __________ you (go) now?" "I _________ (go) to the bus stand."

o) "Where _________ you __________(live)?" "I _________ (live) in Pune."

p) "What __________ you________ (do)?" "I _________ (water) the plants." Generally I _______ (water) these plants on Sunday but I ______________ (do) it a day before because I _________ (go) to Delhi next weekend.

6.9 Answer the following questions orally. The first one has been done as an example:

a) Are you reading a novel? When do you read the textbooks?

Yes, I am (short ans.)/No, I am not (short ans.)

I read the textbooks at …

b) What are you doing here? Do you do this every morning?

c) What do you think about these birds? Are they living in a family like us?

d) Why do they learn English? Are they learning to pass an exam?

e) Where does she come from? Is she teaching you English?

f) Why is he smiling? Does he always smile in the English period?

g) When are they coming home? Do they come home late?

h) Do you understand the difference between Simple Present and Present Continuous? Why are you not listening to the English teacher?

i) Is he coming late to school daily? When does he wake up?

j) Is he dancing now? When does he practise dance?

k) Are you coming to the school by car? Do you use public transport for going to your school?

l) What am I teaching you today? Do you need some more examples?

6.10 Fill in the blanks with either Simple Present or Present Continuous forms of the verbs given in the brackets:

a) Look, I ________ (see) a policeman on the road. He ________ (chase) a man.

b) _______ you (hear) me? Yes, I ____________ (listen).

c) The teacher __________ (ask) the questions now. I __________ (think) Mohan __________ (know) all the answers.

d) The Earth _______ (move) round the Sun.

e) Water ________ (freeze) at 0 degrees. It ______ (boil) at 100 degrees.

f) Which song _________ (sing) he next? He _________ (sing) a Tamil song.

g) It ______ (seem) he ________ (come) from the school now.

h) What ________ (read) you now? I _________ (read) Snake. What _________ (mean) you by this? I _______ (mean), I __________ (read) Snake, a poem, by D H Lawrence.

Present Perfect: has/have + V3

6.11 Answer the following based on the example in the short form given below:

Question : Have you met him?

Answer : Yes, I have seen him / No, I have not seen him. **(Long form)**

Yes, I have / No, I haven't. **(Short form)** ✓

{In the short form the main verb is omitted.}

a) Have you read this novel?

b) Has she been to Delhi?

c) Have you had your breakfast?

d) Have you ever been to a foreign country?

e) Has he understood your instructions?

f) Have you visited the city recently?

g) Has she solved the exercises on Tenses?

h) Have they learned the lesson from this chapter?

i) Has he had lunch?

j) Has he put some sugar?

k) Have you learnt the steps of this dance?

l) Has he taken my pen?

m) Has she given you this gift?

n) Have you kept my book on the table?

6.12 Use the given options to complete two separate sentences: one with *for* and the other with *since*. The examples have been given below for your reference:

Examples:

I haven't eaten any fruits.............

i) four days; ii) last week.

a) I haven't eaten for four days.

b) I have not eaten since last week.

(**Note:** 'since' is used with a point of time in the past and 'for' with a duration/period of time in the past, present or future. For eg. since 1947, for a year.)

a) It hasn't rained here.........
i) months ii) July

b) We haven't watched a movie...........
i) three months ii) January

c) She hasn't spoken to me..........
i) four days ii) Monday

d) I have worn the same dress...........
i) a week ii) last week

e) I haven't been to the city..........
i) last month; ii) two weeks.

f) We haven't had tea................
i) more than a month; ii) we met last.

g) The teacher hasn't taken leave...........
i) months together; ii) December.

h) She hasn't bought her dress...........
i) last year; ii) several months.

i) I haven't listened to my favourite singer.............
i) more than a fortnight; ii) I came here

j) I haven't heard from him............
   i) October; ii) many days

k) They have lived in the colony............
   i) five years; ii) 2012

<u>Present Perfect Continuous</u>: has/have + been + V4

Present Perfect and Present Perfect Continuous

a) He has given the same answer for three days.

b) He has been giving the same answer for three days.

In the first example the action of giving the answer is complete. In the second example the action that began in the past is still continuing.

Present Continuous and Present Perfect Continuous

Examples:

a) He is sitting in the chair.

(Pr Continuous)

b) He has been sitting in the chair for an hour. (Present Perfect Continuous)

The first example (Pr Continuous) indicates that the action is continuing at the present moment, while the second (Pr Perfect Continuous) shows that it started in the past and it still continues.

6.13 Use the verbs in the brackets into Present Perfect Continuous to fill in the blanks:

(Verbs: stay, wait, rest, live, learn, study, lie, stand, sit, sleep, jog, run, walk, watch, look, talk, do, work, read, burn etc.)

a) My mother _______________ (cook) for an hour and we ____________ (wait) for breakfast at the dining table.

b) She ____________ (try) to learn Tamil for the last six months.

c) I ___________ (look) for the book for two days but I am unable to locate it.

d) They ____________ (stay) in this house for a month.

e) The dog ___________ (lie) on the highway.

f) The passengers ______________ (wait) for the train since morning.

g) Our car __________ (pass through) a dense forest.

h) What you ___________ (do) the whole day? I ____________ (read) a novel?

i) She _______________ (work) since 2012.

j) He __________ (talk) about climate change for an hour.

k) My brother _____________ (sleep) since then.

l) The puppies ______________ (play) with one another since morning.

6.14 Fill in either 'since' or 'for' in the following:

a) She has been studying _____ two hours.

b) They have been swimming _______ 7 am.

c) It has been raining ________ yesterday.

d) What have you been doing ________ such a long time?

e) They have not been working together _______ a month.

f) It has been crawling on the sand ________ half an hour.

g) What has she been working at _____ morning?

h) What has he been cooking ________ an hour?

i) They have been trying hard _____ a year.

j) The birds have been singing _______ dawn.

k) The dog has been barking _______ 10 pm.

6.15 Fill in either Present Perfect or Present Perfect Continuous forms of the verbs given in the brackets:

a) The teacher _______________ (explain) Tenses for half an hour but I _______________ (not understand) them yet.

b) Look! The tiger ________ (chase) the deer for the last five minutes but he ______ (not catch) any yet.

c) He __________ (play) for twenty minutes but ________ (not score) a goal yet.

d) She ___________ (write) a story for the last three days but she ________ (not finish) till date.

e) I ___________ (prepare) for the Exams these days, so I __________ (not come) out of the house.

f) The book ___________ (lie) on my desk for several days but I ___________ (not read) a page.

g) They ___________ (chat) on Facebook but they _______ (not meet) each other.

h) He ___________ (not come) back home. That means he ________ (work) still.

i) We ______________ (wait) for the train for four hours but it __________ (arrive).

j) They _________ (not appoint) a new English teacher, though they ___________ (look) for one for the last two months.

Past Tense

Simple Past: V2

6.16 Read/Write the following in a) Simple Past Affirmative and in b) Simple Past Negative. Two examples have been given below:

He brushes the teeth. (Simple Present) →

i) He brushed the teeth. (Simple Past positive)

ii) He did not brush the teeth. (Simple Past negative)

She steals the money. (Simple Present) →

i) She stole the money. (Simple Past positive)

ii) She did not steal the money. (Simple Past negative)

(Verbs: begin, come, learn, teach, do, flow, have, win, choose, know, eat, run, like, ring, break, buy, bring, read, write, hurt, lie, drink, hide, cost, catch, take, throw, go, see, smell, swim, wear, put, make)

a) She learns French.

b) They have a car.

c) You wear a casual dress.

d) He runs away.

e) Aeron spends too much.

f) It crawls on the sand.

g) He goes late.

h) We have an old scooter.

i) Birds fly.

j) Our team always wins.

k) The boys swim.

l) He makes a cup of coffee.

6.17 Read/Write the following as Simple Past questions. The first one has been done as an example:

a) She rang the bell.
Did she ring the bell?

b) Pintu found the book.

c) He lost the bag.

d) The food tasted nice.

e) The teacher smiled.

f) The students laughed.

g) Everybody stood up.

h) The dentist pulled out the tooth.

i) The door opened.

j) The baby cried.

k) They climbed the stairs.

l) He fell to the ground.

m) She hurt her finger.

Types of questions: *Wh* and *Yes/No*

Study the examples below:

a) When did you wake up in the morning? → I woke up at 6 am.

b) Did he come to the school? → Yes, he came / No, he didn't.

As you can see above, the first question (a) is a *Wh* question, while the second (b) is a *Yes/No* question. A *Wh* question starts with a *Wh* word like *who, what, when, where, which, how* etc. The answer to the *Yes/No* question starts with either *Yes* or *No* and it may be in the short form. But the answer to the *Wh* question has a complete sentence.

6.18 Answer the following questions:

a) Did you understand the chapter?

b) When did you watch a movie last time?

c) Where did you buy this mobile?

d) Did you learn to speak English properly?

e) Did your friend tell a lie?

f) How long did you take to finish the homework?

g) What did you have for dinner today?

h) When did he come from the school?

i) What did he learn in English?

j) Did they attend the party?

k) Did she have a smart phone?

l) Where did they go during the summer vacation?

m) How long did we wait for the train?

6.19 Answer the following according to the given question either in Present Perfect or Simple Past tense:

a) Have you been to Shimla?

b) Did you finish the homework?
c) When did he last see a wrestling match?
d) Has she prepared for the Examinations?
e) Where have they gone?
f) How long did it take you to reach the station?
g) Has she had her breakfast?
h) Have they bought a car?
i) How much did it cost?
j) How many matches did your team win?
k) Did Rohan cook the food?
l) Who has shut the door?
m) Where have they hidden the gift?
n) When did he lose his mobile?
o) Did you understand Simple Past Tense?

Past Continuous: was + V4 (ing)

6.20 Change the following into Past Continuous using the time indicators in the brackets. If there are time indicators in the sentences they have to be replaced. Two of them have been done as examples:

Examples:

She is going to the office now. (Yesterday)

She was going to the office yesterday.

They are coming from the market. (last night)

They were coming from the market last night.

a) Renu is doing the homework. (in the evening)
b) We are preparing for the examinations now. (last month)
c) I am reading a novel these days. (last week)
d) They are playing football nowadays. (during that period)
e) Manan is working in the fields. (that day)

f) Nancy and Mehak are going to attend the party. (last fortnight)

g) Shivam is playing the guitar now. (in the morning)

h) I am cycling. (last evening)

Present Continuous is used to express an action in progress in the present, while Past Continuous is used to express an action in progress in the past. In both cases the action is not complete.

Simple Past and Past Continuous

Examples:

i) When she entered the house I read a poem.

ii) When she entered the house I was reading a poem.

In each example given above two actions of the past have been expressed. In example i) the actions take place one after the other in the past: first 'she entered', then 'I read'.

In example ii) one action takes place in the middle of the other in the past: she 'entered' in the middle of 'reading'. The action of 'reading' was still going on then. It was not complete.

6.21 Use Past Continuous tense forms of the verbs given in the brackets to fill in the blanks:

a) He __________ (cook) when I entered the house.

b) They __________ (wait) for the guest when I gave the news.

c) The man broke his knee while he __________ (get down) a bus.

d) I saw the school when I __________ (drive) on the highway.

e) I saw a dolphin while I __________ (swimming) in the Ganga.

f) It took a dip when he __________ (watch) the river.

g) A nightingale __________ (sing) when I woke up.

h) It flew away while she __________ (jog).

i) They heard the noise when they __________ (have) dinner.

j) He got an idea when he __________ (listen) to the teacher.

k) She received the message while she __________ (chat) with her friends.

l) Who ________ (sit) with you when I came?

6.22 Fill in the blanks using the verbs given in the brackets either in Simple Past or Past Continuous:

(Note: Past Continuous is used to express the action in the progress, not its completion)

a) My grandfather ________ (sit) in the Sun when I _________ (meet) him.

b) The woodpecker _________ (look) at her while she _________ (walk).

c) They ________ (have) coffee when the fire ________ (break out).

d) We ________ (watch) TV when we __________ (hear) about the accident.

e) The car ______ (hit) him while he ________ (ride) a bicycle.

f) I _______ (see) the Minister when I ________ (watch) the function.

g) An idea _______ (strike) me when I ________ (write) the story.

h) You ______ (wear) a black shirt when I first _______ (see) you.

i) They _______ (walk) in the rain when they _______ (catch) cold.

j) He _______ (get) hurt while he ________ (run) on the ground.

k) When he __________ (reach) the hotel the function _________ (go on).

l) We _________ (drive) on the road when the car __________ (collide) with the truck.

6.23 The following verbs are generally not used in the Continuous form:

(have, see, hear smell, taste, believe, feel, think, remember, forget, suppose, mean, want, wish, forgive, refuse, love, hate, care, seem, appear, belong to, contain, consist of, possess, own, lose, gain)

Use either Simple Past or Past Continuous forms of the verbs given in the brackets to fill in the blanks:

a) The woman _______ (reading) a book when I first _______ (see) her.

b) Initially I ______ (think) he _________ (play) hockey.

c) While he ________ (perform) the experiment, I ________ (watch) a video.

Past Perfect: had + V3

Past Perfect can best be understood by comparing it with Simple Past. When there are two actions in the past, Past Perfect is used for the action that takes place before, while the Simple Past for the one that happens after.

Example:

The train had left before Sanjay reached the station.

Both the actions took place in the past but the train left the station first, Sanjay reached later. So the Past Perfect has been used for the former and Simple Past for the latter.

6.24 Use either Simple Past or Past Perfect tense forms of the verbs given in the brackets to fill in the blanks:

a) He felt sorry as he ________ (make) a mistake.

b) After she __________ (finish) the work, she went for a walk.

c) Rosie said that she _________ (inform) the police.

d) Munna had run away before the cops ________ (reach) the spot.

e) I went home after she ______ (share) the news.

f) He wondered how the magician _______ (perform) the act.

g) I ________ (understand) Past tense only after I ________ (listen to) the English teacher carefully.

h) When he _______ (deliver) his speech, I ______ (ask) one question.

i) He ________ (arrive) in the school before the function started.

j) The bird ________ (fly) away, before we ________ (click) its picture.

6.25 Use either Simple Past or Past Perfect tense forms of the verbs given in the brackets to fill in the blanks:

a) After she ________ (take) dinner, she ________ (watch) a movie.

b) When she ________ (switch off) the light, she ________ (hear) some noise from outside.

c) I ______ (reach) the station before the train ______ (start).

d) She ________ (say) that she ________ (complete) the homework.

e) My friend ________ (say) that he ________ (build) a new house.

f) He ________ (tell) her that he ________ (cook) the food.

g) The English teacher ________ (ask) the student if he ________ (understand) Past Perfect.

h) The woman ________ (enquire) whether the plane ________ (land).

i) When I _______ (go) there he _______ leave).

j) She _______ (reach) home before the rain _______ (start).

k) The storm _______ (come) after they ______ (finish) the meal.

l) I ______ (wake up) after they ______ (ring) the bell.

Future Tense

Simple Future: will + V1

Simple Future is used to express future time.

6.26 Change the following sentences of Simple Present into Simple Future:

Examples:

He plays the piano → He will play the piano.

I do not/don't go to his place → I will not/won't go to his place.

(do not/don't → won't

does not/doesn't → won't)

a) He tells a lie.
b) I understand your problem.
c) He doesn't speak a word.
d) They always complain.
e) We don't sit idle.
f) John does the homework.
g) She never listens to me.
h) Why don't they work together?
i) They never repair their house.
j) I don't go to the fish market.
k) She hates the rules of grammar.
l) They don't watch movies.

Simple Future: Questions and Answers

***Yes / No* question:**

Q) Will you come to the school tomorrow?

A) Yes, I will/will come (affirmative)

No, I will not/will not come (negative)

***Wh* question:**

Q) When will they reach Mumbai?

A) They will reach Mumbai ...

Note: For the *Wh* question any suitable time reference like tomorrow, *next week, next month* etc. can be added at the end.

6.27 Answer the following questions:

a) Will you come here tomorrow?
b) Will he play for our team?

c) When will she finish the work?

d) Where will we meet next week?

e) Will you teach the tenses again next period?

f) What will she do after breakfast?

g) Will there be a cricket match tomorrow?

h) Will you be present on Monday?

i) When will he go there?

j) Will your mother scold you?

k) Will you come on time?

Shall/Will or Going to

Shall/Will + verb is used in Simple Future to express future time. However the same can be expressed by another verb form like *going to* which is an example of present continuous tense. Let's look at the following examples to understand the difference:

a) i. She will tell the truth.

ii. She is going to tell the truth.

'Going to' is more usual with persons than with 'things'

a) He is going to tell the story in the evening.

b) The water is going to rise in the river tomorrow.

Going to is more appropriate in example (a) with he (person) as the subject, while *will* is more suited for example (b).

6.28 Change the following sentences of Simple Future into Present Continuous with *Going to*:

a) They will perform it tomorrow.

b) I shall meet you on Saturday.

c) She will reach the office by 11:00 a.m.

d) We will have breakfast at 9 a.m.

e) He will leave for Mumbai next week.

f) Ranjan will send his car soon.

g) Madhu will speak next.

h) Will you participate in the competition on Sunday?

i) Will they sing together for the function today?

j) Will she attend the party this afternoon?

k) I shall purchase the books in the fair.

l) Will he arrange for the meeting?

Future Continuous: will/shall + be + V4

Like the other continuous tenses, Future continuous tense is also used to show that the action is in progress in future:

Examples:

He is cooking food. (Pr Continuous)

He was cooking food. (Past Continuous)

He will be cooking food. (Future Continuous)

6.29 Put the following into Future Continuous tense using the time reference given in the brackets:

1. He is working on the project. (next month)
2. The neighbours are helping us. (in the coming month)
3. She is still living in the hostel. (in January)
4. We are playing tennis. (Next week)
5. Mantu is preparing for the exams.
6. Sahil is doing the homework. (tomorrow)
7. Ali is cycling to the school. (next fortnight)
8. I am writing a story. (in the morning)
9. We are constructing a house. (next year)
10. They are buying the gift for his birthday. (next month)
11. She is singing a song. (at 9:00 a.m.)

7.
Adjectives

How to identify?

In the following pairs of sentences the first one has been re-written by including the word given in the brackets:

a) Ranjit drinks water. (cold)

Ranjit drinks **cold** water.

b) Children are playing. (small)

Small children are playing.

In sentence a) *cold* is used before *water,* which is a noun. Similarly in b) *small* is used before *children,* which is again a noun.

7.1 Rewrite the sentences using the words in brackets and underline the nouns before which they are to be used:

a) I met a lady. (kind)

b) Anu buys books. (new)

c) The students are rewarded. (punctual)

d) Several workers are waiting. (poor)

e) She was playing with dolls. (beautiful)

f) Flowers are in the garden. (colourful)

g) You have many friends. (good)

h) Some people gave money. (rich)

i) They saw an elephant. (white)

j) Mother purchased a shirt. (yellow)

k) She is a person. (courageous)

The words in the brackets that are used before the nouns in the above sentences are known as **Adjectives**. They say something about these nouns.

Adjectives: before the nouns or after

In the following examples the adjectives have been used not before the nouns, but after them:

i) The lady was kind.

ii) The apples are green.

Kind is an adjective in i) for the noun, *lady,* but it doesn't come before the noun. It appears after the noun. In the same way *green* is used for apples but is used after the same.

7.2 Rearrange the jumbled words below to form meaningful sentences. Then underline the adjectives and circle the nouns for which they have been used:

a) kind was lady the

b) new are books the

c) are the punctual students

d) several are workers poor

e) beautiful she dolls the gave are

f) garden are the colourful in flowers my

g) all friends his are good

h) gave money the who people the rich are

i) was one only elephant white

j) shirt mother my the purchased yellow is

k) courageous is person met the I

Adjectives are used for nouns in two different positions in sentences: **before a noun** (attributive) and **after a noun** (predicative). The same adjective may be used sometimes before a noun, sometimes after as in the following examples:

It is a large building →	*Large* (adjective) has been used before building (noun). So it is an attributive adjective.
The building is large →	*Large*, is again used as an adjective here but it is after the noun, building. It is known as a predicative adjective.
A tall woman is coming →	*Tall* is an attributive adjective as it has been used before the noun, woman.
The woman is tall →	Here *tall* is a predicative adjective. It comes after the noun.

7.3 Rearrange the jumbled words below to form meaningful sentences. Underline the adjectives and write if they are used before the noun (attributive) or after the noun (predicative):

a) has high Majid fever

b) sentence is a it correct

c) questions the are easy

d) a it story long is

e) bought Sunder market grapes the black from

f) teacher difficult my always questions asks

g) meeting enjoy people I young

h) obedient the were students

i) bags were their heavy

j) lost important were papers my

k) Suman famous Delhi met people in

l) old she the sang songs are

m) in bird small garden in my sitting the is

n) cooked he tasty the has food is

The intensity of Adjectives

7.4 Rewrite the sentences using the given words at the appropriate places:

Very, quite, rather, completely, extremely, unusually, really, fairly

a) She is intelligent.

b) This is a wrong answer.

c) Ram is bright.

d) The milk is warm.

e) You are correct.

f) It is a false story.

g) He is a bad boy.

h) This is a large building.

i) A tall lady came to our house.

The words before the adjectives in the sentences above have been used to increase or decrease the intensity of these adjectives. So these words (very, quite, rather, completely, extremely etc.) are called **intensifiers**.

Adjectives for Comparison

The following examples show how adjectives can change their forms for comparison:

Renu is <u>tall</u>. →	**Tall** (there is no comparison)
Bhumi is <u>taller</u> than Renu. →	**Tall+er** (comparison between two persons)
Ram is the <u>tallest</u> in the class →	**Tall+est** (comparison among three or more)
Ali is as <u>tall</u> as John →	**Tall** because the degree of comparison is between the two persons of similar degree.

7.5 Fill in the appropriate forms of the adjectives given in the brackets:

a) Cats are ______ than rats. (big)
b) Vegetables are ____ than Fruits. (cheap)
c) Sonu is the _____ girl in the school. (tall)
d) This building is as ____ as that one. (high)
e) Look at the ____ star in the sky. (bright)
f) Anju's hair is _____ than Manju's hair. (long)
g) Sanjay is the ____ of all. (clever)
h) His bag is _____ than my bag. (heavy)
i) She is the _____ lady in the colony. (old)
j) Bhairav is as ____ as Mohan. (thin)
k) Ali is ____ than Krishna. (happy)
l) Her dress is the ____ in the group. (pretty)
m) July is ____ than September. (hot)
n) December is as ____ as January. (cold)
o) This exercise is ____ than the previous one. (easy)

In the above exercise all the adjectives have three forms like

big	bigger	biggest
long	longer	longer
clever	cleverer	cleverest
easy	easier	easiest

→ The first(base) form is called **positive**, the second with *er* is known as **comparative** and the third, with *est*, **superlative**.

→ all the adjectives above are changed to comparative by adding *er* and superlative form by adding *est*.

→ in adjectives like easy and pretty the last letter y is replaced by *ier* for comparative and *iest* for superlative.

Regular and Irregular Adjectives

A small group of common adjectives do not change their forms with the regular *er* or *est* for comparison. The examples are as follows:

a) Manju is a good student.

Urjit is better than Manju.

Ali is the best among the three.

b) The day was as bad as any other.

Yesterday was worse than before.

Today is the worst day of my life.

Some more examples are:

Good - better - best,

bad - worse - worst

Little - less - least

Less - lesser - least

Many - more - most

Much - more - most

→ The adjectives (big, small, tall, sad, kind etc.) that change their forms with *er* or *est* for comparison are known as **Regular Adjectives** and those (good, bad etc.) which do not change with *er* or *est* are called **Irregular Adjectives**.

7.6 Choose the correct form of the adjectives from the brackets to fill in the blanks:

a) The ____ day of the week is Sunday. (better, best, good)

b) Summer is ______ than winter. (worse, worst, bad)

c) My brother was _____ than his friends in Chess. (better, good, best)

d) Do you think this movie is the _____ of all? (worse, bad, worst)

e) As a city Mumbai is as _____ as Delhi. (worst, worse, bad)

f) I am not as _____ in English as she is. (worse, bad, worst)

g) Cricket is the _____ of all the outdoor games. (bad, worse, worst)

h) He is the ____ student in the class. (best, good, better)

Where to use *More* and *Most*?

In the following examples the adjectives do not change their forms for comparison. Instead *more* and *most* are used for comparison:

a) This is an interesting book.

This book is *more* interesting than that.

This book is the *most* interesting of all.

b) Ramu is intelligent.

Shyamu is *more* intelligent than Ramu.

Birju is the *most* intelligent of all.

7.7 Use the adjectives in the brackets to fill in the blanks. *More* or *most* can be used before them according to the requirement:

a) This room is as _________ as that one. (comfortable)

b) Mangoes are ___________ than apples. (tasteful)

c) This is the ___________ plant among all in my garden. (beautiful)

d) He is the __________ person of the three members in my family. (handsome)

e) The movie was _________ than the book. (enjoyable)

f) Ganga becomes the ___________ of all the rivers in the rainy season. (dangerous)

g) This is a very _________ lesson. (important)

h) Motorbikes are ________ than bicycles. (expensive)

i) He is __________ than his friend. (careful)

j) Gold is the ___________ of all the metals. (valuable)

k) Sanju is as _________ as Sonu. (careless)

Which adjectives should change their form and which ones should use *more* or *most* for comparison? The answer lies in the length of the adjectives. Generally shorter ones (big, long, sad, short etc.) change their forms, while longer ones (beautiful, important, comfortable etc) take *more* or *most*.

Examples:

1. The car is lighter than the motorbike.

   The car is more comfortable than the motorbike.

2. She is the tallest student in the class.

   She is the most intelligent student in the class.

In the first pair of sentences light is short in length, so it changes its form with *er* for comparative, while comfortable is longer, so it uses *more*. Similarly tall changes its form with *est*, while intelligent takes *most* for superlative.

7.8 Use the adjectives in the brackets to fill in the blanks. You may change their form or use more or most for comparison according to the requirement:

a) This is the __________ (beautiful) of all the four pictures.

b) Chinese is ______ (difficult) than Hindi.

c) Amir Khan is as ______ (popular) as Shahrukh Khan.

d) Everest is the ______ (high) peak in the world.
e) Table tennis is _______ (enjoyable) than Chess.
f) She is ______ (good) at Spanish than her friend.
g) This is the _______ (boring) book that I have read.
h) A dog is the ________ (faithful) animal in the world.
i) I am __________ (bad) at Maths than my friend.
j) Mangoes are ___________ (healthy) than cakes.
k) Gorkhas are the _________ (courageous) of the soldiers.
l) Blood is _______ (thick) than water.
m) The USA is the _________ (prosperous) country in the world.
n) Ramesh is __________ (brilliant) than Raju.
o) Umesh is the ________ (brilliant) student in the class.
p) He is as _______ (foolish) as his brother.
q) But Gunjan is the __________ (foolish) of them all.
r) The weather is _________ (hot) than yesterday.
s) Peace is always ________ (good) than a war.

8.
Adverbs

8.1 Rearrange the following to make sentences. The first one has been done as an example:

a) he happily lived

He lived happily.

b) slowly she walks

c) sat quietly Mother

d) watched I silently

e) Meenu loudly spoke

f) him told politely I

g) comes she late usually

h) she rudely speaks

i) quickly finished the they work

j) solved he problem the easily

k) we moving carefully were

Each sentence here has a word ending with *ly* like happily, slowly, quietly, silently etc. They are used after the verbs. They also say something about the verbs. So they are called **Adverbs.**

For example, *happily* in a) says about the way *he lived. Slowly* in b) says about the way *she walked.*

Adverbs of manner

8.2 Fill in the blanks adding *ly* to the words given in italics. The first one has been done as an example:

a) Her song is *beautiful.*

She sings *beautifully.*

b) Dad was a *careful* driver.

Dad drove _______.

c) She was a *wonderful* teacher.

She taught ________.

d) He is a *marvellous* painter.

He paints ________.

e) My friend was *slow.*

My friend walked ______.

f) Rohan was *quiet.*

Rohan sat _______.

g) She is *loud.*

She speaks ______.

h) He is *fluent.*

He speaks ______.

i) They are *polite.*

They behave _____.

j) She is *frank.*

She told me ______.

In the first pair *beautiful* is an adjective which says something about the noun, *song.* When *ly* is added to *beautiful,* it becomes an adverb and it says something about the verb, *sings.*

In each pair the adverb is formed by adding *ly* to the given adjectives:

careful → carefully

wonderful → wonderfully

marvellous → marvellously

slow → slowly

quiet → quietly

loud → loudly

fluent → fluently

polite → politely

frank → frankly

Each adverb indicates how an action is performed:

Carefully for the manner of driving, *wonderfully* for the manner of teaching, *slowly* for the manner of walking etc.

So the adverbs that end in *ly* are called **adverbs of manner**.

Adverbs of time

Adverbs not only indicate only the manner of the actions performed. They also tell the time of the actions. Look at the adverbs in the following examples:

She came yesterday.

He spoke now.

Both the adverbs, *yesterday* and *now,* tell about the verbs, *came* and *spoke,* which they follow respectively. They describe when the actions were performed.

So they are known as **adverbs of time**.

Examples:

Yesterday, tomorrow, today, now, then, early, late, still, yet, soon, after, before

8.3 Arrange the following words to make sentences. Underline adverbs of time in each:

a) Reshu yesterday reached

b) today met he

c) finished early she

d) we late arrived

e) are tomorrow guests going

f) came after I

g) met have they before

h) they playing now are football

i) sending I am you gift a soon

j) she tell then will me

Adverbs of place

8.4 Arrange the following words to make sentences. Underline the adverbs of place in each:

a) stay there will we

b) here come you

c) came she in

d) He up went

e) boy the off fell

f) fell Jack down

g) Grandmother near sat me

h) went she out

i) reached we home

j) Ganesh out came

k) Ankit below stood

l) I above saw the monkey

Each adverb tells something about the verb in the sentence. It tells where the action is performed.

So they are called **adverbs of place**.

Examples:

here, there, out, in, outside, inside, home, up, down, indoors, back, near, far, everywhere, above, below, off, nearby, under

Adverbs of frequency

8.5 Use the adverbs in the brackets in the sentences:

a) He plays Chess. (always)

b) I meet him. (usually)

c) We argue. (never)

d) She is on time. (generally)

e) They are finishing the work. (just)

f) I am watch the stars. (sometimes)

g) Sudha saw her. (often)

h) They will return. (never)

i) I am helping him. (always)

j) She is late. (sometimes)

Each adverb used in the above exercise tells how often the action is performed.

So they are called **adverbs of frequency**.

Examples:

sometimes, always, never, often, just, now, generally, usually etc.

Note:

Adverbs of manner, time or place are generally used after the verb, at the end of the sentence. However, adverbs of frequency are used before the Main Verbs in sentences. If there are Auxiliary Verbs in the sentences, then they are used after the Auxiliary Verbs.

9.

Prepositions

The underlined words in the following examples are known as **Prepositions**:

i) The watchman is *at* the gate.

ii) My father is *on* the roof.

iii) My brother is *in* the bedroom.

Each Preposition above is placed before a noun. *At* before gate, *on* before roof and *in* before bedroom.

A **Preposition** is a word used before a noun or a noun phrase.

Prepositions of place

9.1 Fill in the blanks using the prepositions of place, *in, at, on* in the following:

[at – point, on – surface, in – area]

a) The cat was waiting _____ the door.

b) There was a fire _____ the building.

c) The book is ______ the table.

d) I saw my face _____ the mirror.

e) The ring was _____ the pocket.

f) He met me ______ the station.

g) Her bag was lying ______ the floor.

h) The car is ______ the road.

i) My father is ______ the house.

j) The bird is ______ the garden.

Prepositions of movement

9.2 Fill in each of the following prepositions only once in each blank:

(across, among, by, in, at, between, to, on)

between
A ——— B

among
ABC —— PQR

towards
——→

a) We went _____ the hotel.

b) He went ______ the road.

c) I saw the label _____ the packet.

d) She came ______ car.

e) My house is _____ a village.

f) Nepal lies _______ India and China.

g) He is the best player ______ the boys.

h) The shop is _____ the corner.

Prepositions of direction

9.3 Use the following prepositions to fill in the blanks:

(up, down, over, under, above, behind, in front of, before, after)

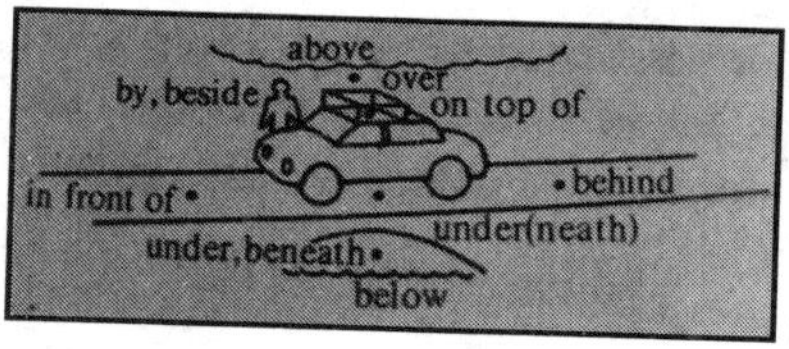

a) A comes ______ B but D comes _____ C.

b) P is over T, so T must be ______ P.

c) The plane was flying ______ the city.

d) If my house is behind the temple, then the temple is ______ my house.

e) There was a blanket _____ his body. The shoes were ______ the bed. ______ the bed a clock was hung.

f) He went _____ the hill by car but came ______ walking.

g) The passenger was sitting in front of me, I was sitting ______ him.

9.4 Fill in the prepositions in the following blanks:

(to, towards, by, through, from, into)

a) Last month we were going _____ Goa ______ Mangalore ______ train.

b) In the morning the train started moving away ______ the station.

c) The train had to pass ______ several tunnels.

d) It also went ______ a number of bridges.

e) Going ______ a tunnel was very enjoyable.

f) Whenever it went ______ a tunnel we were excited.

Prepositions of time

9.5 Use the following prepositions to fill in the blanks:

(at, in, on, for, since, during, after, before, until, by)

a) He was born _____ November.

b) I go to school _____ 8 am.

c) We went to the market ______ Sunday.

d) They went to a hill station _____ a week.

e) She was waiting _____ evening.

f) The students were silent _____ the lecture.

g) He will reach home _____ 10 pm.

h) We can't come back _____ late evening.

i) The train will come _____ an hour.

j) I can't reach _____ time.

9.6 Fill in the blanks with mixed types of prepositions for place, movement, direction, time etc.:

a) The bus came _____ time.

b) It started _____ Chandigarh _____ the afternoon _____ 2 pm.

c) He dived _____ the river.

d) The aeroplane was flying _____ the sea.

e) He travelled _____ road.

f) She is _____ the classroom.

g) I have been calling you _____ morning.

h) I parked the bicycle _____ the gate _____ 8 am.

i) We both met _____ the beach _____ Tuesday.

j) The man came there fifteen minutes _____ the time. His friend came late. He came an hour _____ that.

k) Every morning we walk _____ the track _____ an hour.

l) We bought some popcorn _____ interval.

10.

Conjunctions

The underlined words in the following sentences are known as ***Conjunctions***:

i) Ram <u>and</u> Ali are friends.

ii) The homework is difficult <u>but</u> enjoyable.

iii) Would you like tea <u>or</u> coffee?

In i) *and* joins Ram with Ali. It is used to join similar ideas.

In ii) *but* joins *difficult* with enjoyable. It is used to join opposing ideas.

In iii) *or* joins tea with coffee. It is used to join alternate ideas.

Conjunctions are used to join two or more than two words. They are also used to join two or more than two sentences.

10.1 Use *and, but, or* to fill in the blanks in the following:

a) Is the Taj Mahal in Agra ______ Delhi?

b) I met his brother ______ sister.

c) Do you like Football _____ cricket?

d) She was happy _______ tired.

e) He saw me _________ smiled.

f) Would you have juice ______ soup?

g) Peter _____ John are friends.

h) They were poor ______ honest.

i) I bought apples ______ oranges.

j) He was cheerful ______ strict.

10.2 Fill in each of the blanks with one word. Do not use a word twice.

[mother, India, intelligent, tea, enjoyable, vegetables, went, indoor, discussed, tiring]

a) Would you have _____ or coffee?

b) My father and ______ are in Canada.

c) The movie is long but ______.

d) Is she in ______ or China?

e) I bought _____ and fruits.

f) He is _____ but naughty.

g) We met and ______ the problem.

h) Do you like _____ or outdoor games?

i) The journey was pleasant but _______.

j) I _____ and met him.

In the above exercise *and*, *or*, *but* are the conjunctions that have been used to join words in sentences. They can also be used to join sentences:

i) Sonal is intelligent.

Her brother is hardworking.

Sonal is intelligent and her brother is hardworking.

ii) He is good in studies.

His marks are low.

He is good in studies but his marks are low.

iii) I want food.

I can't work.

I want food or I can't work.

10.3 Combine each pair into one sentence using *and*, *or*, *but*:

(a) Ram got the first prize.
Mohan got the second.

(b) I was in the room.
I didn't see him.

(c) Please tell the truth.
I will not help you.

(d) We reached on time.
he had left.

(e) She came to the school.
She met me.

(f) Switch off the lights.
He will be disturbed.

(g) Put on a jacket.
You will catch a cold.

(h) The teacher was teaching.
The student was sleeping.

(i) Mother cooks the food.
I serve it.

(j) Juhi is reading Maths.
She hates it.

11.

Negatives and Questions

11.1 Use the auxiliaries to change the following into negative sentences. One has been done as an example:

(is, are, am, was, were, has, have, had, will, shall, would, should, can, may)

a) Karan is running. Karan is not running.

b) Hemant was ill.

c) Meena was crying.

d) They have bought the house.

e) We shall win.

f) We had finished the work.

g) You were present.

h) She will speak.

i) They are telling the truth.

j) The truck has stopped.

k) You can do.

l) I am happy.

m) Suresh is absent.

n) They should help.

11.2 Change the above negative sentences into their short forms:

Example:

Karan is not running. → Karan isn't running.

11.3 Use the auxiliaries to change the following sentences into questions. One has been done as an example.

a) He has come. → Has he come?

b) She is in the class.

c) They had complained.

d) Sibu was talking.

e) Mehul can play.

f) We are waiting.

g) He will agree.

h) I may come.

i) You have broken the chair.

j) She was laughing.

k) We were silent.

Do/ Does/ Did

The following sentences do not have auxiliary verbs. They are changed into negatives with the help of the auxiliaries; *do*, *does* and *did*.

i) He *eats* apples. → He *does not eat* apples.

ii) He *ate* apples. → He *did not eat* apples.

iii) They *eat* apples. → They *do not eat* apples.

When the main verb ends with 's'(eats), then *does* is used for the negative and 's' is removed from the main verb(eat).

When the main verb is in the first form(eat), then *do* is used for negative. The main verb remains the same(eat).

When the main verb is in the second form(ate), *did* is used for the negative and the main verb is changed to the first form(eat).

11.4 Change the following into negatives:

a) The ice melted.

b) She scolds her brother.

c) Renu lay awake.

d) Students come here.

e) They build a house.

f) A man stands at the gate.

g) Birds flew away.

h) The team played yesterday.

i) He cooked the food.

11.5 Use *do, does* or *did* to change the following sentences into questions:

a) They reached the station.

b) Mehar asks a question.

c) Sonali cut her finger.

d) He sent a card.

e) Raheem listens to her.

f) They chat with the passengers.

g) She shouted at him.

h) He shut down the computer.

i) The cat drinks milk.

j) They celebrate the festival.

11.6 The following sentences are mixed. Some of them use auxiliary verbs, while others are without auxiliaries. Change them into negatives:

a) She hit the ball.

b) They have told lies.

c) Anjali kept the book.

d) My mother bought a smartphone.

e) He has been watching the match.

f) I had met the cop.

g) We were swimming in the pool.

h) He has a guitar.

i) They have the answer.

j) I was singing a song.

k) He shuts the door.

11.7 Change the following into negative questions. Further write the short forms of these negative questions. The first one has been done as an example:

a) He is flying kites. →

Is he not flying kites? →

Isn't he flying kites?

b) They are rowing a boat.

c) She put a notebook in the bag.

d) She has a tablet.

e) Jugnoo saw me.

f) Naseer eats oranges.

g) Rohan stayed there.

h) Urja stopped the car.

i) They were walking.

j) You finished the work.

k) We have reached the bus stand.

Answer key

1. Nouns

1.1

Each sentence begins with a noun.

1.2

a) occur
b) spills
c) hoot
d) jump
e) shines
f) march
g) burns
h) burns

1.3

a) play / study
b) shouts / smiles / cries
c) passes

d) fall
e) shouts / smiles / cries
f) bite
g) shouts / smiles / cries
h) play / study
i) grows
j) sticks

1.4

naming, action, verbs, with

2. Types of Nouns

2.1

b) boy - C, Ravi - P
c) village - C, Jaito - P
d) Shilpa - P, Girl - C
e) Asia - P, continent - C
f) company- C, Tata - P
g) India - P, country - C
h) student - C, Mehak - P
i) Priti - P, teacher - C
j) Roshan - P, player - C
k) Sherpur - P, village - C
l) town - C, Barh - P
m) David - P, photographer -C
n) Junaid - P, worker - C
o) Mitthu - P, parrot - C

2.2

c) Horses run.

d) Not possible
e) Birds sing.
f) Not possible
g) Students speak.
h) Not possible
i) Not possible
j) Days begin.
k) Not possible

2.3

two, Proper, Common, one, two, Common, Proper

2.4

b) Not possible
c) Farmers walk.
d) Tigers sleep.
e) Not possible
f) Not possible
g) Trains move.
h) Mangoes fall.
i) Not possible
j) Not possible

2.5

two, Countable, one, Uncountable

2.6

a) apple, apples
b) elephant, elephants
c) snake, snakes

d) soldier, soldiers
e) passenger, passengers
f) train, trains
g) insect, insects
h) day, days
i) bell, bells

2.7

a) woman, women
b) clock, clocks
c) goose, geese
d) box, boxes
e) kid, kids
f) orange, oranges
g) child, children
h) bush, bushes
i) sheep, sheep
j) ox, oxen
k) leaf, leaves

2.8

a) A mother is a woman.
b) A bird is a creature.
c) A market is a place.
d) A brinjal is a vegetable.
e) A wife is a woman.
f) A child is a human being.
g) An ox is an animal.
h) A mouse is a living being.

i) A deer is a wild animal.

j) A teacher is a human being.

k) A clock is a machine.

l) A fly is an insect.

2.9

a) Obama loves an orange.

b) A student plays chess.

c) A goat gives milk.

d) A pen requires ink.

e) A painter uses paint.

f) A snake eats a frog.

g) A house needs furniture.

h) A sheep eats grass.

i) A gentleman attends a party.

j) A tooth needs care.

k) A lady wears a *saree*.

l) A man wears a *dhoti*.

m) A fish lives in water.

n) A baby likes a toy.

o) A cow feeds a calf.

p) A deer eats a plant.

q) Teddy drinks coffee.

r) A factory creates pollution.

s) Maruti produces a car.

t) Google gives an app.

u) Pollution affects a city.

v) A flood hits India.

3. Pronouns

3.1

a) He

b) I, you, He, She, They, They

c) It, She, She, it, they

d) You, I, he, he, He, She, They, They, He, She

e) You, I, you, We

f) I, I, I, She, We, It, We, It, They

3.2

b) We

c) him

d) her

e) I

f) us

g) them

3.3

b) I

c) you

d) it

e) us

f) they

g) we

h) them

i) me

j) you

k) him

3.4

b) He, them
c) She, them
d) It, them
e) We, them
f) They, us
g) He, her
h) They, him
i) We, it
j) They, him
k) He, us

3.5

a) They are writing.
b) They are speaking.
c) I am trying.
d) He/She is eating.
e) You are laughing.
f) They are crawling.
g) We are coming.
h) I am running.
i) He/She is coming.
j) They are singing.

4. Determiners

4.1

a) a, an, the, the
b) this, that, these, those

c) a, my, its
d) two, a, a, The, Its, the, his, their
e) my, this, their, the, a, their
f) his, Her, her, their, The, a

Articles

4.2

a) An elephant is an animal.
b) A hospital is a building.
c) An ant is a creature.
d) A goose is a bird.
e) A man is a human being.
f) A verb is a word.
g) A car is a vehicle.
h) An Indian is an Asian.
i) A cat is a pet.
j) An apple is a fruit.
k) A computer is a machine.
l) An ox is a male.
m) A thief is a criminal.

4.3

a) X
b) X
c) a
d) an
e) X
f) X

g) X

h) a

i) X, X

j) X

k) a, a

l) a

m) X

n) X, a

o) an

p) X, an

q) a, a

r) X, X

s) X

t) a, a

u) X, an

v) an, a, X

w) X, a

4.4

Proper, Plural, Uncountable

4.5

a, an – Indefinite (I)

the – Definite (D)

4.6

a) a, the

b) the

c) an, the

d) the, the
e) a, an
f) a, the
g) a, the
h) a, a, the, the, the
i) a, the

4.7

a) the
b) X
c) X, X
d) X, X, the
e) X, X
f) the, the
g) the
h) the
i) the
j) the
k) the, the
l) the
m) the

4.8

a) a dog, a goat, a cat
b) bought yesterday
c) brothers
d) eldest
e) our school, had come
f) died of old age

g) because he was ill
h) three friends
i) elderly gentleman on the platform
j) set a record in the Board Exams

4.9

a) the, the
b) the, the
c) the, the, the, the
d) the, the
e) the, X
f) X, X
g) the, X, the
h) X, the
i) the, the, The, X, the, X
j) the, X, the

Other Determiners

4.10

a) this
b) this, that
c) That
d) this, that
e) this, that
f) that
g) this
h) this, that
i) that
j) this, that

4.11

a) These stories are very interesting.
b) I like those movies.
c) Those boxes are heavy.
d) These boys have broken those chairs.
e) Those fans are quite old.
f) Those students will sit here but these students will sit there.
g) Those elephants have broken these plants.
h) He is waiting for those gentlemen.
i) She meets these pedestrians.
j) These chapters are easier than those ones.

4.12

a) some
b) any
c) some
d) any
e) some
f) some, any
g) any
h) any
i) some

4.13

a) any
b) some
c) any
d) some
e) any

f) any

g) some

h) any

i) some

Note: Some , affirmative, any, negative

4.14

a) a few

b) a little

c) a few

d) a few

e) a few

f) a little

g) a little

h) a few

i) a little

j) a little

Note: number , amount

4.15

a) many

b) much

c) many

d) many

e) much

f) many

g) many

h) much

i) many

j) many
k) much
l) many
m) many
n) much

Note: much, amount, many, number

4.16

a) few
b) a few
c) few
d) a little
e) little
f) a little
g) a little
h) a few
i) little
j) little
k) a few

4.17

a) much
b) many
c) a few
d) a little
e) little/much
f) many
g) many
h) a little
i) a few

4.18

a) student
b) animals
c) hour
d) evening
e) information
f) money
g) children
h) members
i) parents
j) dogs
k) book
l) brothers/sisters

4.19

b) i Det
ii Pr
c) i Det
ii Pr
d) i Pr
ii Det
e) i Det
ii Pr
f) i Pr
ii Det
g) i Pr
ii Det
h) i Det
ii Pr

i) i Det

ii Pr

j) i Det

ii Pr

5. Verbs

5.1

a) Babies are not crying.

b) Ramu should not study.

c) They have not reached.

d) Mehar is not cooking.

e) Sameer has not played.

f) Girls are not shouting.

g) You were not sleeping.

h) I am not walking.

i) He might not return.

j) She will not explain.

k) Kabir was not swimming.

l) Mohan had not told me.

5.2

a) Is Raji standing?

b) Are they coming?

c) Can she read it?

d) Has Mukul gone?

e) Have they finished the work?

f) May he speak?

g) Was Renu running?

h) Were dogs barking?

i) Will they do it?

j) Is he listening?

5.3

a) are - AV, watching - MV

b) started - MV

c) sing - MV

d) was - AV, running - MV

e) told - MV

f) will - AV, come - MV

g) may - AV, go - MV

h) crawls - MV

i) should - AV, begin - MV

j) ring - MV

k) were - AV, chatting - MV

l) has - AV, arrived - MV

m) have - AV, fallen - MV

n) must - AV, get - MV

o) play - MV

p) can - AV, do - MV

q) dance - MV

5.4

a) is

b) have

c) does

d) are

e) is

f) am

g) has

h) is

i) do

5.5

c) X

d) X

e) sent

f) X

g) say

h) X

i) travelling

j) reached

5.6

It is an open-ended exercise. Only the Main Verb should be in its first form with a Modal Auxiliary.

5.7

a) had

b) is

c) has (even a modal can be used)

d) do

e) are

f) are

g) can/should/must (any of them)

h) can/should/must (any)

i) does/did

j) must/should

k) does/did

l) has/had

m) have

5.8

a) I called him.

b) They opened the door.

c) They danced well.

d) The parents hugged her.

e) We decorated the house.

f) The students shouted.

g) My teachers advised me.

h) I accepted the gift.

i) They closed the gate.

j) You behaved well.

5.9

a) They sent a gift.

b) I read a book.

c) I felt bad.

d) We bought fruits.

e) You threw the garbage.

f) The parents came.

g) They left early.

h) We met in the park.

i) She cut her finger.

j) I slept at 10.

5.10

a) become
b) think/thought
c) feed
d) love
e) building
f) started
g) shut
h) sleep
i) admitted
j) close
k) kept
l) accepted
m) decorating
n) melts
o) removed

5.11

a) made
b) tells/told
c) answered
d) singing
e) looks
f) working
g) leaving
h) become
i) hit

5.12

a) thinking - Irregular
b) looking - Regular
c) gave - Irregular
d) asked - Regular
e) find - Irregular
f) seems - Regular
g) trying - Regular
h) leaving - Irregular
i) want - Regular
j) see - Irregular
k) take - Irregular
l) coming - Irregular
m) going - Irregular
n) told - Irregular
o) work - Regular
p) feel - Irregular
q) say - Irregular

6. Tenses

6.1

a) present tense - past time
b) present tense - past and present time
c) future tense - future time
d) present tense - past, present and future time
e) present tense - past, present and future time
f) past tense - past time

g) present tense - future time
h) present tense - past time

6.2

a) present perfect
b) past continuous
c) present continuous
d) simple present
e) past perfect
f) present perfect continuous
g) simple future
h) past perfect continuous
i) simple past
j) future continuous
k) future perfect
l) future perfect continuous

6.3

a) Yes, he is cooking.
No, he is not cooking.

b) Yes, I am standing.
No, I am not standing.

c) Yes, you are speaking loudly.
No, you are not speaking loudly.

d) Yes, they are listening.
No, they are not listening.

e) Yes, she is driving.
No, she is not driving.

f) Yes, Reshu is waiting.
No, Reshu is not waiting.

g) Yes, you are going.
No, you are not going.

h) Yes, you are reading correctly.
No, you are not reading correctly.

i) Yes, I am writing an email.
No, I am not writing an email.

j) Yes, she is running.
No, she is not running.

k) Yes, they are living here.
No, they are not living here.

l) Yes, we are working together.
No, we are not working together.

6.4

a) She is writing …
b) He is reading …
c) We are going to …
d) He is eating …
e) I am coming from …
f) They are speaking …
g) We are carrying …
h) She is …
i) I am listening to …
j) They are cutting …
k) I am standing at …
l) I am taking …
m) He is making …

Simple Present

6.5

a) He goes to school at …
b) They chat during …
c) I read the textbooks at …
d) She sings during …
e) He dances at …
f) We meet at …
g) Rohan completes homework at …
h) We discuss at …
i) Shweta plays hockey at …
j) We have dinner at…
k) I brush my teeth at …
l) He teaches at …
m) My mother calls me at …
n) They ask questions in …
o) He talks to his friends at …

Note: The ending of each answer in this has been kept blank. It can be filled according to the choice. Even the preposition in each has more than one option.

6.6

a) My daughter plays an indoor game.
b) His friend likes chicken.
c) He/She does not like fish.
d) This lady travels by bus.
e) Her parent does not attend the meeting.
f) He/She lives in a big house.

g) The bird builds its nest.

h) The man stays at home, while the woman goes out for work.

i) The teacher scolds the student sometimes.

j) The driver drives the bus fast.

k) The passenger always arrives late.

6.7

a) The student starts for school in the morning. He/She attends a class, listens to his/her teacher, chats with his/her friend and comes back home in the afternoon. In the evening he/she again goes back for tuition and comes back tired and exhausted. He/She doesn't get the time for a game or self study.

b) This boy goes shopping everyday. He purchases a vegetable and a fruit but he does not buy an item like pizza or a burger.

c) Nowadays the child enjoys playing a mobile game. He/She hardly ever goes to the park for an outdoor game. It is no surprise then that he/she suffers from a life-style disease.

d) He/She has a banana for breakfast, and I have a *chapati*. For lunch he/she has rice, and I have *daliya*.

e) My cousin studies till late in the night. So he does not wake up early in the morning. I finish my work in the evening. So I wake up early.

6.8

a) rises

b) is watching

c) sings, is singing

d) think, is swimming

e) comes, is coming

f) cooks, is cooking

g) is reading, plays

h) allows

i) build

j) is crying, wants

k) belongs, is buying

l) meet, am meeting

m) is coming, works

n) are you going, am going

o) do, live

p) are you doing, am watering, water, am doing, am going

6.9

b) I am playing.
Yes, I do / No, I don't.

c) I think they are beautiful.
Yes, they are. / No, they aren't.

d) They learn English to…
Yes, they are. / No, they aren't.

e) She comes from France.
Yes, she is. / No, she isn't.

f) He is smiling because…
Yes, he does. / No, he doesn't.

g) They are coming home at …
Yes, they do. / No, they don't.

h) Yes, I do / No, I don't.
I am not listening to the English teacher because…

i) Yes, he is. / No, he isn't.
He wakes up at…

j) Yes, he is / No, he isn't.
He practises at…

k) Yes I am. / No, I am not.
Yes, I do. / No, I don't.

l) You are teaching…
Yes, we do. / No, we don't.

6.10

a) see, is chasing
b) Do you hear, am listening
c) is asking, think, knows
d) moves
e) freezes, boils
f) is he singing, is singing
g) seems, is coming
h) are you reading, am reading, do you mean, mean, am reading

6.11

a) Yes, I have. / No, I haven't.
b) Yes, she has/ No, she hasn't.
c) Yes, I have. / No, I haven't.
d) Yes, I have. / No, I haven't.
e) Yes, he has. / No, he hasn't.
f) Yes, I have. / No, I haven't.
g) Yes, she has. / No, she hasn't.
h) Yes, they have. / No, they haven't.
i) Yes, she has. / No, she hasn't.
j) Yes, he has / No, he hasn't.
k) Yes, I have. / No, I haven't.
l) Yes, he has. / No, he hasn't.

m) Yes, she has. / No, she hasn't.

n) Yes, I have. / No, I haven't.

6.12

a) It hasn't rained here for months.
It hasn't rained here since July.

b) We haven't watched a movie for three months.
We haven't watched a movie since January.

c) She hasn't spoken to me for 4 days.
She hasn't spoken to me since Monday.

d) I have worn the same dress for a week.
I have worn the same dress since last week.

e) I haven't been to the city for two weeks.
I haven't been to the city since last month.

f) We haven't had tea for more than a month.
We haven't had tea since we met last.

g) The teacher hasn't taken leave for months together.
The teacher hasn't taken leave since December.

h) She hasn't bought her dress for several months.
She hasn't bought her dress since last year.

i) I haven't listened to my favourite singer for more than a fortnight.
I haven't listened to my favourite singer since I came here.

j) I haven't heard from him for many days.
I haven't heard from him since October.

k) They have lived in the colony for 5 years.
They have lived in the colony since 2012.

6.13

a) has been cooking, have been waiting

b) has been trying

c) have been looking
d) have been staying
e) has been lying
f) have been waiting
g) has been passing through
h) have you been doing, have been reading
i) has been working
j) has been talking
k) has been sleeping
l) have been playing

6.14

a) for
b) since
c) since
d) for
e) for
f) for
g) since
h) for
i) for
j) since
k) since

6.15

a) has been explaining, have not understood
b) has been chasing, has not caught
c) has been playing, has not scored
d) has been writing, has not finished

e) have been preparing, have not come

f) has been lying, have not read

g) have been chatting, have not met

h) has not come, has been working

i) have been waiting, has not arrived

j) have not appointed, have been looking

Past Tense

Simple Past

6.16

a) She learnt French.
She did not learn French.

b) They had a car.
They did not have a car.

c) You wore a casual dress.
You did not wear a casual dress.

d) He ran away.
He did not run away.

e) Aeron spent too much.
Aeron did not spend too much.

f) It crawled on the sand.
It did not crawl on the sand.

g) He went late.
He did not go late.

h) We had an old scooter.
We did not have an old scooter.

i) Birds flew.
Birds did not fly.

j) Our team always won.
Our team did not always win.

k) The boys swam.
The boys did not swim.

l) He made a cup of coffee.
He did not make a cup of coffee.

6.17

b) Did Pintu find the book?

c) Did he lose the bag?

d) Did the food taste nice?

e) Did the teacher smile?

f) Did the students laugh?

g) Did everybody stand up?

h) Did the dentist pull out the tooth?

i) Did the door open?

j) Did the baby cry?

k) Did they climb the stairs?

l) Did he fall to the ground?

m) Did she hurt her finger?

6.18

a) Yes, I did. / No, I didn't.

b) I watched a movie last time in…

c) I bought this mobile …

d) Yes, I did. / No, I didn't.

e) Yes, he did. / No, he didn't.

f) It took 5 minutes/…

g) I had rice/*chapatis*/…

h) He came at …
i) He learnt …
j) Yes, they did. / No, they didn't.
k) Yes, she had. / No, she hadn't.
l) They went to …
m) You waited for …

6.19

a) Yes, I have been to. / No, I haven't been to.
b) Yes, I did. / No, I didn't.
c) He saw it in …
d) Yes, he has. / No, he hasn't.
e) They have gone to …
f) It took …
g) Yes, she has. / No, she hasn't.
h) Yes, they have. / No, they haven't.
i) It cost …
j) Our team won … matches.
k) Yes, he did. / No, he didn't.
l) X has shut the door.
m) They have hidden it in the …
n) He lost his mobile in the …
o) Yes, I did. / No, I didn't.

6.20

a) Renu was doing the homework in the evening.
b) We were preparing for the examinations last month.
c) I was reading a novel last week.
d) They were playing football during that period.

e) Manan was working in the fields that day.
f) Nancy and Mehak were going to attend the party last fortnight.
g) Shivam was playing the guitar in the morning.
h) I was cycling last evening.

6.21

a) was cooking
b) were waiting
c) was getting down
d) was driving
e) was swimming
f) was watching
g) was singing
h) was jogging
i) were having
j) was listening
k) was chatting
l) was sitting

6.22

a) was sitting, met him
b) looked, was walking
c) were having, broke out
d) were watching, heard
e) hit, was riding
f) saw, was watching
g) struck, was writing
h) were wearing, saw
i) were walking, caught

j) got, was running
k) reached, was going
l) were driving, collided

6.23

a) was reading, saw
b) thought, was playing
c) was performing, was watching

6.24

a) had made
b) had finished
c) had informed
d) reached
e) had shared
f) had performed
g) understood, had listened
h) had delivered, asked
i) had arrived
j) had flown away, clicked

6.25

a) had taken, watched
b) switched off, heard
c) had reached, started
d) said, had completed
e) said, had built
f) told, had cooked
g) asked, had understood

h) enquired, had landed
i) went, had left
j) had reached, started
k) came, had finished
l) woke up, had rung

6.26

a) He will tell a lie.
b) I will understand your problem.
c) He won't speak a word.
d) They will always complain.
e) We won't sit idle.
f) He will do the homework.
g) She will never listen to me.
h) Why won't they work together?
i) They will never repair their house.
j) I won't go to the fish market.
k) She will hate the rules of grammar.
l) They won't watch movies.

6.27

a) Yes, I will. / No, I won't.
b) Yes, he will. / No, he won't.
c) She will finish the work/it by …
d) We will meet at …
e) Yes, I will. / No, I won't.
f) She will …
g) Yes, there will be. / No, there won't be.

h) Yes, I will be. / No, I won't be.
i) He will go there …
j) Yes, she will. / No, she won't.
k) Yes, I will. / No, I won't.

Note:

1. The answers for *Yes/No* questions have been given only in the short form. But even the long ones may be accepted.

   For example the long one for a) will be

   Yes, I will come. / No, I won't come.

2. The blank at the end of the answer for a *Wh* question is open ended. Multiple options may be used for one blank. For example the options for c) morning/evening/10 am etc. So the complete answer may be as follows:

   She will finish the work/it by morning/evening/10 am.

6.28

a) They are going to perform it tomorrow.
b) I am going to meet you on Sunday.
c) She is going to reach the office by 11:00 a.m.
d) We are going to have breakfast at 9:00 a.m.
e) He is going to leave for Mumbai next week.
f) Ranjan is going to send his car soon.
g) Madhu is going to speak next.
h) Are you going to participate in the competition on Sunday?
i) Are they going to sing together for the function today?
j) Is she going to attend the party this afternoon?
k) I am going to purchase the books in the fair.
l) Is he going to arrange the meeting?

6.29

1. He will be working on the project next month.
2. The neighbours will be helping us in the coming month.
3. She will still be living in the hostel in January.
4. We shall/will be playing tennis next week.
5. Mantu will be preparing for the exams.
6. Sahil will be doing the homework tomorrow.
7. Ali will be cycling to the school next fortnight.
8. I shall/will be writing a story in the morning.
9. We shall/will be constructing a house next year.
10. They will be buying the gift for his birthday next month.
11. She will be singing a song at 9:00 am.

7. Adjectives

7.1

a) I met a kind lady.
b) Anu buys new books.
c) The punctual students are rewarded.
d) Several poor workers are waiting.
e) She was playing with beautiful dolls.
f) Colourful flowers are in the garden.
g) You have many good friends.
h) Some rich people gave money.
i) They saw a white elephant.
j) Mother purchased a yellow shirt.
k) She is a courageous person.

7.2

a) The lady was kind.
b) The books are new.
c) The students are punctual.
d) Several workers are poor.
e) The dolls she gave are beautiful.
f) The flowers in my garden are colourful.
g) All his friends are good.
h) The people who gave the money are rich.
i) Only one elephant was white.
j) The shirt my mother purchased is yellow.
k) The person I met is courageous.

7.3

a) Majid has a <u>high</u> fever. — before the noun
b) It is a <u>correct</u> sentence. —- before the noun
c) The questions are <u>easy</u>. —- after the noun
d) It is a <u>long</u> story. —- before the noun
e) Sunder bought <u>black</u> grapes from the market. —-- before the noun
f) My teacher always asks <u>difficult</u> questions. —-- before the noun
g) I enjoy meeting <u>young</u> people. —-- before the noun
h) The students were <u>obedient</u> —- after the noun
i) Their bags were <u>heavy</u>. —-- after the noun
j) My <u>important</u> papers were lost. —-- before the noun
k) Suman met <u>famous</u> people in Delhi. —-- before the noun
l) The songs she sang are <u>old</u>. —-- after the noun

m) The <u>small</u> bird is sitting in my garden. —-- before the noun

n) The food he cooked is <u>tasty</u>. —-- after the noun

7.4

a) She is extremely intelligent.

b) This is a completely wrong answer.

c) Ram is quite bright.

d) The milk is fairly warm.

e) You are quite correct.

f) It is a completely false story.

g) He is a very bad boy.

h) This is an unusually large building.

i) A very tall lady came to our house.

Note: The intensifiers used above are not absolute. The same intensifier may be used with more than one adjective.

7.5

a) bigger

b) cheaper

c) tallest

d) high

e) brightest

f) longer

g) cleverest

h) heavier

i) oldest

j) thin

k) happier

l) prettiest

m) hotter
n) cold
o) easier

7.6

a) best
b) worse
c) better
d) worst
e) bad
f) bad
g) worst
h) worst

7.7

a) comfortable
b) more tasteful
c) most beautiful
d) most handsome
e) more enjoyable
f) most dangerous
g) important
h) more expensive
i) more careful
j) most valuable
k) careless

7.8

a) most beautiful
b) more difficult

c) popular
d) highest
e) more enjoyable
f) better
g) most boring
h) most faithful
i) worse
j) healthier
k) most courageous
l) thicker
m) most prosperous
n) more brilliant
o) most brilliant
p) foolish
q) most foolish
r) hotter
s) better

8. Adverbs

8.1

b) She walks slowly.
c) Mother sat quietly.
d) I watched silently.
e) Meenu spoke loudly
f) I told him politely.
g) She comes late usually.
h) She speaks rudely.
i) They finished the work quickly.

j) He solved the problem easily.

k) We were moving carefully.

8.2

b) carefully

c) wonderfully

d) marvellously

e) slowly

f) quietly

g) loudly

h) fluently

i) politely

j) frankly

8.3

a) Reshu reached yesterday.

b) He met today.

c) She finished early.

d) We arrived late.

e) Guests are going tomorrow.

f) I came after.

g) They have met before.

h) They are playing football now.

i) I am sending you a gift soon.

j) She will tell me then.

8.4

a) We will stay there.

b) You come here.

c) She came <u>in</u>.

d) He went <u>up</u>.

e) The boy fell <u>off</u>.

f) Jack fell <u>down</u>.

g) Grandmother sat <u>near</u> me.

h) She went <u>out</u>.

i) We reached <u>home</u>.

j) Ganesh came <u>out</u>.

k) Ankit stood <u>below</u>.

l) I saw the monkey <u>above</u>.

8.5

a) He always plays chess.

b) Usually I meet him.

c) We never argue.

d) She is generally on time.

e) They are just finishing the work.

f) I watch the stars sometimes.

g) Sudha often saw her.

h) They will never return.

i) I am always helping him.

j) Sometimes she is late.

9 Prepositions

9.1

a) at

b) in

c) on

d) in
e) in
f) at
g) on
h) on
i) in
j) in

9.2

a) to
b) across
c) on
d) by
e) in
f) between
g) among
h) at

9.3

a) before, after
b) under
c) above
d) in front of
e) over, under, above
f) up, down
g) behind

9.4

a) from, to, by
b) from

c) through
d) through
e) through
f) into

9.5

a) in
b) at
c) on
d) for
e) since
f) during
g) by
h) until
i) after
j) before

9.6

a) on
b) from, in, at
c) into
d) above
e) by
f) in
g) since
h) at, at
i) on, on
j) before, after
k) on, for
l) during

10.1

a) or
b) and
c) or
d) but
e) and
f) or
g) and
h) but
i) and
j) but

10.2

a) tea
b) mother
c) enjoyable
d) India
e) vegetables
f) intelligent
g) discussed
h) indoor
i) tiring
j) went

10.3

a) Ram got the first prize and Mohan the second.
b) I was in the room but I didn't see him.
c) Please tell the truth or I will not help you.

d) We reached on time but he had left.
e) She came to the school and met me.
f) Switch off the lights or he will be disturbed.
g) Put on the jacket or you will catch a cold.
h) The teacher was teaching but the student was sleeping.
i) Mother cooks the food and I serve it.
j) Juhi is reading Mathematics but she hates it.

11. Negatives and Questions

11.1

b) Hemant was not ill.
c) Meena was not crying.
d) They have not bought the house.
e) We shall not win.
f) We had not finished the work.
g) You were not present.
h) She will not speak.
i) They are not telling the truth.
j) The truck has not stopped.
k) You cannot do.
l) I am not happy.
m) Suresh is not absent.
n) They should not help.

11.2

b) Hemant wasn't ill.
c) Meena wasn't crying.
d) They haven't bought the house.

e) We shan't/won't win.
f) We hadn't finished the work.
g) You weren't present.
h) She won't speak.
i) They aren't telling the truth.
j) The truck hasn't stopped.
k) You can't do.
l) I ain't happy.
m) Suresh isn't absent.
n) They shouldn't help.

11.3

b) Is she in the class?
c) Had they complained?
d) Was Sibu talking?
e) Can Mehul play?
f) Are you waiting?
g) Will he agree?
h) May I come?
i) Have I broken the chair?
j) Was she laughing?
k) Were you silent?

11.4

a) The ice did not melt.
b) She does not scold her brother.
c) Renu did not lie awake.
d) Students do not come here.
e) They do not build a house.

f) A man does not stand at the gate.
g) Birds did not fly away.
h) The team did not play yesterday.
i) He did not cook the food.

11.5

a) Did they reach the station?
b) Does Mehar ask a question?
c) Did Sonali cut her finger?
d) Did he send a card?
e) Does Raheem listen to her?
f) Do they chat with the passengers?
g) Did she shout at him?
h) Did he shut down the computer?
i) Does the cat drink milk?
j) Do they celebrate the festival?

11.6

a) She did not hit the ball.
b) They have not told lies.
c) Anjali did not keep the book.
d) My mother did not buy a smartphone.
e) He has not been watching the match.
f) I had not met the cop.
g) We were not swimming in the pool.
h) He does not have a guitar.
i) They do not have the answer.
j) I was not singing a song.
k) He does not shut the door.

11.7

b) Aren't they rowing a boat?
c) Didn't they put a notebook in the bag?
d) Doesn't she have a tablet?
e) Didn't Jugnoo see me?
f) Doesn't Naseer eat oranges?
g) Didn't Rohan stay there?
h) Didn't Urja stop the car?
i) Weren't they walking?
j) Didn't I finish the work?
k) Haven't you reached the bus stand?

Bibliography

1. Leech, G., Svartvik, J. (1973), A Communicative Grammar of English
2. Tickoo, M., L., Subramanian, A., E., (1977), A Functional Grammar with Usage and Composition
3. Quirk, R., Greenbaum, S. (1973), A University Grammar of English
4. Quirk, R., Greenbaum, S., Leech G., Svartvik, J. (2010), A Comprehensive Grammar of the English Language
5. Allen, W. S., (2009), Living English Structure